SLOW COOKING

ALL YEAR ROUND

SLOW COOKING

ALL YEAR ROUND
Great-tasting meals with minimum fuss

Jessica Cole

NH
NEW HOLLAND

Contents

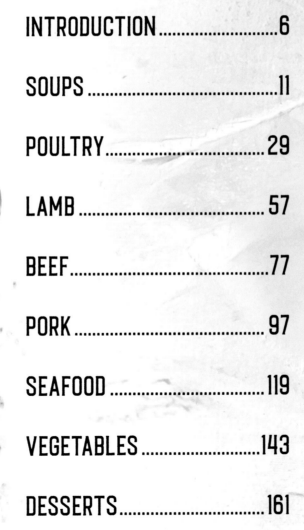

INTRODUCTION

All foods, as we know, are prone to seasonal change. This is because our food histories and cultural eating practices usually originate from the land, from the simple beginnings of subsistence farming and peasant cookery. There is, however, another kind of food seasonality – different foods come in and out of favor according to the fashions of the time.

What was in fashion 10 years ago is different from what is in vogue today. The fascinating part of the current change in food perceptions is the return of many of the old ways of cooking. Fast food has definitely been put in its place and a return to slow food is very much back in the public's perception of what is both good for you and what is presentable at the table. Within the idea that some of the old ways of cooking are truly worthy and should be enjoyed alongside quick meals, speedy salads and wok-tossed minute meals, there is a strong place for the slow and hearty fireside foods of old.

The slow-cooking pot that bubbled away for hours on the edge of the fireplace made a successful electronic conversion in the late 60s and early 70s and became the 'crockpot'.

Like most fashions, crockpots were heartily embraced and people realised that an appliance that could slow-cook a wet meal automatically (usually without the need for stirring or watching over) was a convenient way to produce wonderful traditional family meals without being tied to the kitchen for the entire day. The crockpot has, however, like many food innovations become identified with the time of its invention and is now seen as old technology. Ask your mum and she probably still has one stashed in the back of her cupboard somewhere or under the preserving equipment gathering dust in the back shed. It will likely be beige or burnt orange in color with a motif on the side – a testament to the time of its previous popularity.

These cookers have recently had a makeover and with the resurgence of interest in slow food and traditional cooking techniques they are perfectly placed to again be seen with pride bubbling away on the side of the kitchen bench, imparting beautiful aromas to your kitchen while happily cooking, unaided and unsupervised.

Traditional slow-cooked soups, continental casseroles, hearty stews and exotic tagines – the traditional and slow foods from all nations – are back on the food agenda and the poetic and provincial idea of slow cooking inexpensive cuts of meat is seen at some of the finest eateries around the Western world. In short, the slow cooker is back, looking good and ready for service in the modern kitchen.

Once you have started cooking with a slow cooker you will soon realise its convenience and economy. The slow cooker is a low-fuss appliance that is also a low-energy user – once the cooker reaches core temperature the mass of the food helps to retain its own heat and very little extra heat is needed to maintain temperature. Flavors are trapped inside the cooking environment and each component imparts its character and takes on the flavors of what is around it. Good quality stocks, fresh vegetables, citrus rinds and robust flavors such as rosemary and thyme are the winning elements to beautiful old-fashioned cookery.

One of the labor- and time-saving elements of this style of cooking is the fact that you can create the ultimate cooking short cut by cutting up your meats and vegetables and adding them to the one pot (your slow cooker) – the only things to wash are your cutting board and knife. The rest is taken care of from cooking to serving, leaving you with only the ceramic insert and the dinner plates for the after-dinner wash-up. There are few simpler and more fundamental ways of cooking.

GETTING TO KNOW YOUR SLOW COOKER

The various makes of slow cookers respond a little differently to each other so you'll need to gauge cooking time for yourself from the first couple of recipes you try out – if your cooker is particularly large or lower powered then you may need to add a little extra cooking time than the recipe indicates.

For the first few recipes mark down your starting and finishing time so that you quickly get a feel for how your particular slow cooker responds. Keep an eye on your slow cooker in the late stages of cooking to see if it requires any more or less cooking time or a top-up of liquid.

Your slow cooker is exactly that and cannot recover heat losses quickly, so lift the lid only when instructed. If you feel you must remove the lid several times, remember to extend the cooking time a little. You will learn whether to add extra time by simply looking at your meal in the late stages of cooking.

Due to the unique wraparound heating system, low temperature and long cooking periods, slow cooker temperatures cannot be accurately compared to an oven or a frypan (see conversions on page 9). Cooking settings on most slow cookers are LOW and HIGH. Food will be brought to simmer on all settings. The LOW and HIGH settings determine the time needed to reach a simmer. Avoid sudden temperature changes when using your slow cooker as it will not be able to withstand them. Do not put in frozen or very cold foods if the ceramic bowl has been preheated or is hot to the touch.

The removable ceramic bowl may be used in the oven and is ideal to use when adding a pastry crust to your favorite stews. Be careful not to place the ceramic bowl on the range surface or burners.

Your slow cooker can help you get the best advantage from your freezer. You can prepare double the usual quantity of a favorite casserole and when cooked, freeze the extra amount. The best way to freeze food for later reheating is to turn it out from the slow cooker after cooking to allow the ceramic insert to cool. Then wash the ceramic insert and coat it with a little oil or butter before returning the cooled food to it. Cover the ceramic insert and freeze until the food is set. Once set, turn out the block of frozen food and transfer it to a large freezer bag. Then when you return the food to the slow cooker for reheating, it will always fit back in perfectly. Do not use the ceramic bowl for storing food in the freezer indefinitely, and always remember that you cannot return frozen foods to a preheated cooker. When you want a slow-cooked meal without any preparation at all, just place the frozen food into the cooker and heat for 5 to 8 hours. The slow, gentle heating from the cooker will not dry out the meal you are reheating.

You can prepare a recipe the night before in the removable ceramic bowl and store it in the refrigerator so that when you are ready to cook the bowl can be transferred to the slow cooker heating base unit. Just make sure that the base unit has not been preheated. Cook on the desired setting for a little more time than given in the recipe.

Most vegetables should be cut into small pieces, or at least quartered, and placed near the sides and bottom of your cooker. Carrots and other dense root vegetables should be peeled and put where they will be covered by liquid.

An unusual characteristic of the slow cooker is that meats generally cook faster than most root vegetables. The heating element of the slow cooker runs around the outer edges of the insert and because of this it is a good idea to arrange vegetables towards that area.

Small food portions can be cooked in the slow cooker, but the times will vary. Because there is no direct heat at the bottom always fill the cooker at least half full to conform to the recommended times. Adjust your recipe volume according to the size of your slow cooker.

Roasts can be cooked on low without adding water, but a small amount of water is recommended because the gravies are especially tasty and it would be a shame to leave them behind.

The more fat or marbling the meat has, the less liquid you will need as the natural fats in the food help to baste and moisten the finished food.

Since the liquid content of meats and vegetables will vary, you may end up with a recipe with too much liquid. The excess can be reduced by removing the cover and setting the cooker on high for about 45 minutes. Most recipes cooked in the slow cooker will be juicier since the slow cooking prevents evaporation. Your slow cooker should never be filled higher than 2 cm (¾ in) from the top. If it is too full the lid will lift while the food is cooking.

With the high setting, if by chance your dish of food does dry out, do not simply add cold liquid; it is best to boil the kettle and add some extra water, or if you have extra stock, heat it in a small saucepan before adding to the slow cooker.

It is advisable to generally always preheat your slow cooker for 10 to 15 minutes before use. This helps food come up to cooking temperature faster.

GRAVY

- Remove the foods from the pot, leaving the juices.
- Prepare a smooth paste of about 60 g (2 oz) plain flour or cornflour to 60 ml (2 fl oz) water.
- Pour mixture into the liquid in your cooker and stir well.
- Turn to high and cook, stirring occasionally, until mixture thickens and becomes slightly transparent (approximately 15 to 20 minutes). Then it is ready to serve.

ADAPTING YOUR FAVORITE RECIPES FOR THE SLOW COOKER

Here are a few basic hints which will help when you come to adapt other recipes.

- Allow sufficient cooking time on low setting.
- Follow the conversion guide given on the next page.
- Do not add as much water as conventional recipes indicate.

Always cook with the cover on. Your slow cooker cooks best if left undisturbed. Lifting the lid can lengthen the cooking time; if you need to stir your dish, do it during the last few hours of cooking time or only when instructed in the recipe.

Generally, 250 to 500 ml (½ to 1 pint) of liquid are enough for any recipe unless it contains rice, pasta or other absorbing grains such as polenta, couscous or quinoa. The other exceptions are pot roast-style dishes where you expect to have liquids at the end and classic Italian styled 'bolito-misto' dishes where you boil and simmer meats and discard the cooking liquid at the end of the cooking process. In the case of the pot roast, any vegetables and the main joint of meat can be lifted out at the end of its cooking time with a slotted spoon and tongs. Then, with the addition of thirsty grains such as those mentioned above, thick and wet rustic-style gruels can be made to form a magnificent base for a truly old-fashioned meal – simply turn the cooker to high, add some grains and cook for 45 minutes with the lid removed (while the main meat is rested and carved).

Slow cooking is one-step cooking – many steps in conventional recipes may be deleted. You can add all ingredients to the slow cooker at one time and cook for approximately 8 hours.

There are three important exceptions: milk, sour cream and fresh cream should be added during the last half hour of cooking.

When cooking with herbs and spices, whole herbs and spices are preferable. When a recipe calls for dried beans, the beans should be soaked overnight, then cooked on high for 2 to 3 hours. Or you can cook them overnight on low with water and 1 small teaspoon of bicarbonate of soda (baking soda) added to speed up the breakdown of the beans. Instead of soaking or cooking overnight, they may also be parboiled first. When a crisp topping of crumbs or grated cheese is called for, transfer food from the slow cooker to a platter and brown it either with a torch or in the oven. The removable bowls with some models are versatile, as they can be easily put in the oven to achieve the desired topping.

If cooked rice is called for, stir raw rice in with other ingredients. Add 250 ml (8 fl oz) of extra liquid per cup of raw rice. Use long-grain rice for best results in all-day cooking.

Some foods do not benefit from slow cooking, so do not use any of the following unless the recipe says so:
- Crisp-cooked green vegetables
- Noodles
- Macaroni
- Asian vegetables
- Puddings or sauces made with a foundation of milk or cream

Although these foods are familiar favorites, care must be taken when using them in slow cooker recipes.

You can cook without liquid. For example, fish and sausages can be placed in the cooker, covered, and cooked for 2 to 4 hours, depending on the thickness of the meat. You can scrub and dry new potatoes and arrange them in the cooker, cover, and cook for 8 to 10 hours.

GET INVENTIVE

With the guidelines in this introduction you should be able to take any appropriate recipe and convert it to a slow-cooking recipe.

Think outside the square and make the slow cooker work for you. Anything from a hearty porridge with dried fruit slowly cooked overnight to feed a family when it rises for a chilly winter breakfast or preparing a late sweet snack that cooks away as you settle in front of the television after the evening meal – the applications and variations are virtually unlimited.

COOKING TIME CONVERSION GUIDE

This guide applies particularly to casseroles. Most meat and vegetable combinations will require at least 7 hours on low.

All cookers consume approximately the same amount of power. The settings vary according to the make and size and individual style of each cooker, so if you are buying a new cooker, choose wisely and consider your potential end needs.

You can buy cookers with ceramic containers permanently fixed into the outer casings, where the heating elements are placed between the outer casing and the cooking pot. Some of these styles come with detachable power cords so that the entire unit can be taken to the table to serve from.

OVEN OR STOVE TOP	SLOW COOKER	SLOW COOKER
Cooking time	Low cooking time	High cooking time
15–30 mins	4–6 hrs	1½–2½ hrs
35–45 mins	6–8 hrs	3–4 hrs
50 mins–3 hrs	8–12 hrs	4–6 hrs

Another style of cooker has a removable inner ceramic cooking container, which means that only the cooking pot is taken to the table. This style of slow cooker enables food to be easily browned or crisped under the grill for final presentation. In these cookers the heating elements are fitted within the walls of the base unit that the ceramic container fits into.

There are different capacity cookers that vary from 1.5 to 5.5 litres (3 to 11 pints). While the little cookers seem kind of nifty and compact, it is best to get the largest size that you think you can use – once you become familiar with this appliance you will see the benefit of cooking double quantities and large joints of meat. It allows for greater versatility and is an easy way to feed a large number of guests.

TYPES OF COOKERS

All of the slow cookers on the market vary in shape, size and volume capacity. When choosing one there are many considerations to ponder.

HOW TO CLEAN AND CARE FOR YOUR SLOW COOKER

Safety
When using electrical kitchen appliances, basic safety precautions should always be followed.
- Never submerge the slow cooker cooking unit in water. Remove the ceramic bowl and place the bowl in the dishwasher or wash with hot soapy water as soon as possible after emptying it.
- Do not pour in cold water if the ceramic bowl is hot. When cleaning your slow cooker do not use abrasive cleaning compounds. A cloth, sponge or rubber spatula will usually remove the residue. If necessary, a plastic cleaning pad may be used.
- To remove water spots and other stains, use a non-abrasive cleaner or vinegar.
- The metal liner may be cleaned with a damp cloth or scouring pad, or sprayed lightly with an all-purpose cleaner to maintain.
- The outside of the slow cooker may be cleaned with soft cloth and warm soapy water and wiped dry. Do not use abrasive cleaners on the outside.
- Care should be taken to avoid hitting the ceramic pot with metal spoons or water taps. Do not put frozen or very cold foods in the slow cooker if the unit has been preheated or is hot to the touch.
- Read all instructions and become thoroughly familiar with your slow cooker.
- Do not touch hot surfaces; always use handles or knobs.
- Caution must be used when moving the slow cooker if it contains hot oil or other hot liquids.
- Close supervision is necessary when the slow cooker is used by or near children.
- Unplug the slow cooker from the power outlet when not in use, before putting on or taking off parts, and before cleaning.
- Use your slow cooker on an even and stable surface.
- Do not place slow cooker units on or near a hot gas or electric burner, or in a heated oven. Only the ceramic inserts should be placed in the oven or under a grill

SOUPS

SWEET POTATO AND ROSEMARY SOUP

SERVES 4–6

INGREDIENTS

2 tablespoons olive oil

2 cloves garlic, crushed

1 medium onion, chopped

3 tablespoons chopped fresh rosemary

2 tablespoons puréed semi-dried tomato

1 medium carrot, sliced

1 large potato, sliced

700 g (1½ lb) sweet potato, sliced

1 L (2 pt) chicken stock

salt and freshly ground black pepper

METHOD

. Heat the oil in a saucepan, add the garlic, onion and one-third of the rosemary, and cook on a medium heat for 5 minutes. Add the semi-dried tomato purée and cook for 1 minute.

. Add the carrot, potato and sweet potato, and cook for a further 6 minutes.

. Transfer to the slow cooker set on high and add the stock and salt and pepper. Cook for 5 hours, or until the vegetables are soft.

. Purée the soup in a food processor, then return to the slow cooker. Add the remaining rosemary and heat through before serving.

SAVORY PUMPKIN SOUP

SERVES 6–8

INGREDIENTS

1 kg (2.2 lb) pumpkin, peeled, diced

400 ml (13 fl oz) canned tomato juice

1 tablespoon raw sugar

2 L (4 pints) water

salt and freshly ground black pepper

1 bay leaf

few drops of Tabasco sauce

2 chicken stock cubes

125 ml (4 fl oz) pouring cream

2 tablespoons chopped fresh parsley

METHOD

. With the exception of parsley and cream, combine all ingredients in a slow cooker and cook for 6½ hours on low.

. Remove bay leaf. Process the mixture a cupful at a time in a food processor.

. Return mixture to slow cooker and reheat for 15 minutes. Add cream and allow to warm through.

. Serve sprinkled with fresh parsley.

PORCINI MUSHROOM SOUP

SERVES 6

INGREDIENTS

1 tablespoon dried porcini
  mushrooms
125 ml (4 fl oz) boiling water
2 tablespoons olive oil
2 cloves garlic, crushed
1 leek, sliced
6 French shallots, chopped
285 g (9 oz) white mushrooms,
  thinly sliced
500 g (17½ oz) forest
  mushrooms, including shiitake,
  oyster and Swiss brown, thinly
  sliced
2 tablespoons plain flour
1 L (2 pints) good quality
  chicken, beef or vegetable stock
250 ml (8 fl oz) double cream
½ bunch fresh flat-leaf parsley,
  chopped
30 fresh basil leaves, shredded
1 tablespoon fresh oregano
salt and freshly ground black
  pepper
ground nutmeg

METHOD

. Add the dried porcini mushrooms to the boiling water and set aside. When the mushrooms have softened, remove them from the liquid and set aside. Strain the mushroom liquid through a muslin-lined sieve to separate sand and grit, and reserve the liquid.

. Heat the olive oil in a large saucepan and add the garlic, leeks and shallots and cook for about 3 minutes. Add the fresh mushrooms and cook over a very high heat until the mushrooms soften and their liquid evaporates (about 7 minutes). Reserve a few mushroom pieces for the garnish.

. Transfer the leek and mushroom mixture to a preheated slow cooker set on high, then sprinkle with the flour and stir well to enable the flour to be absorbed. Add the stock and the porcini mushrooms together with the reserved liquid. Stir to combine. Cook for 2 hours.

. Add the cream, then turn to low and cook for a further 30 minutes or until slightly thickened. Add half the parsley and the basil and oregano and season to taste with salt and freshly ground black pepper. To serve, ladle into individual bowls sprinkle with extra parsley, reserved mushrooms, some nutmeg and a small dollop of extra cream if desired.

CHICKEN AND CORN SOUP

SERVES 6–8

INGREDIENTS

1 whole cooked chicken (boned, skin removed and chopped into small pieces)

800 g (1 lb 10 oz) creamed corn

2 L (4 pints) chicken stock

salt and freshly ground black pepper to taste

METHOD

. Place all ingredients in slow cooker. Cook covered for 2–3 hours on low or 1–2 hours on high.

Note: This hearty and healthy soup is perfect for those cold winter days.

SAVORY BEAN SPINACH SOUP

SERVES 6

INGREDIENTS

1.25 L (2½ pints) vegetable stock

430 ml (14 fl oz) tomato purée

450 g (16 oz) canned white beans,
   rinsed and drained

125 g (4 oz) cooked rice

½ onion, finely chopped

2 cloves garlic, minced

1 teaspoon dried basil

¼ teaspoon salt

¼ teaspoon freshly ground black
   pepper

8 cups fresh spinach leaves,
   coarsely chopped

5 tablespoons Parmesan cheese,
   grated

METHOD

. Combine stock, tomato purée, beans, rice, onion, garlic, basil, salt
   and pepper in the slow cooker.

. Cover and cook on low for 5–7 hours or on high for 2½–3½
   hours.

. Stir spinach into soup and serve with Parmesan cheese.

SEAFOOD CHOWDER

SERVES 4

INGREDIENTS

500 g (18 oz) fish fillets (bream, snapper, cod or salmon)

125 g (4 oz) bacon, diced

1 medium onion, chopped

4 medium potatoes, peeled and cubed

1 teaspoon salt, or to taste

¼ teaspoon freshly ground black pepper

375 ml (12 fl oz) evaporated milk

METHOD

. Cut fish into bite-size pieces. In a heavy-based frypan, sauté bacon and onion until meat is cooked and onion is golden.

. Drain and put into slow cooker with the fish pieces. Add potatoes, 2 cups of water, salt and pepper.

. Cover and cook on low for 5–8 hours. Add evaporated milk during last hour.

Note: A chowder is a stew or thickened soup. It can be served as a meal on it's own or as a starter. It is especially good when mopped up with crusty bread.

INDIAN SPICED POTATO AND ONION SOUP

SERVES 4

INGREDIENTS

1 tablespoon vegetable oil

1 onion, finely chopped

1 cm (½ in) piece fresh ginger, peeled, finely diced

2 large potatoes, cut into 1 cm pieces

2 teaspoons ground cumin

2 teaspoons ground coriander (cilantro)

½ teaspoon ground turmeric

1 teaspoon ground cinnamon

2 tablespoons cold water

1 L (2 pints) chicken stock

salt and freshly ground black pepper

1 tablespoon natural yoghurt to garnish

METHOD

. Heat the oil in a large saucepan. Cook onion and ginger for 5 minutes or until softened. Add the potatoes and cook for another 5 minutes, stirring often.

. Mix the cumin, coriander, turmeric and cinnamon with cold water to make a paste. Add to the onion and potatoes and fry for 2 minutes, stirring well to release flavors.

. Transfer the potato and spice mixture to a heated slow cooker set on a high setting. Add the stock and season to taste. Bring to the simmer and cover, then cook for 3 hours or until the potato is tender. Blend until smooth in a food processor or with a hand-held blender. Return to the slow cooker and heat through, then adjusting the seasoning again. Before serving garnish with the yoghurt and more pepper.

. Serve with warm naan bread and salad.

TOMATO, LENTIL AND BASIL SOUP

SERVES 4

INGREDIENTS

125 g (4 oz) brown lentils

1 kg (2.2 lb) Roma tomatoes

2 onions, diced

**2 tablespoons sun-dried tomato
purée**

3 cups vegetable stock

1 bay leaf

freshly ground black pepper

60 g (2 oz) fresh basil, chopped

METHOD

. Rinse the lentils, drain and add them to a large saucepan of boiling water. Simmer, covered, for 25 minutes or until tender, then drain, rinse and set aside.

. Meanwhile, place the tomatoes in a bowl, cover with boiling water and leave for 30 seconds, then drain. Remove the skins, deseed and chop.

. In a slow cooker on high, add the onions and stir in the tomatoes, tomato purée, stock, bay leaf and pepper. Cover and simmer for 2¼ hours.

. Remove and discard the bay leaf, then purée the soup until smooth in a food processor or with a hand-held blender. Stir in the lentils and chopped basil, then return to the slow cooker and reheat on high until heated through. Serve garnished with the fresh basil leaves.

CHICKEN SOUP

SERVES 6

INGREDIENTS

1 whole chicken, about 1¼ kg
    (2½ lb)
400 g (14 oz) canned diced
    tomatoes
2 potatoes, diced
2 carrots, diced
1 onion, diced
500 ml (1 pint) chicken stock
juice of 1 lemon
3 cloves garlic crushed
salt and freshly ground black
    pepper
1 teaspoon dried basil
1 teaspoon dried thyme
1 teaspoon dried oregano
½ teaspoon chilli flakes
125 ml (4 fl oz) white wine
400 g (14 oz) canned chickpeas,
    drained and rinsed
400 g (14 oz) canned four bean
    mix

METHOD

. Put chicken in the slow cooker with tomatoes, potatoes, carrot, onion, stock, lemon juice, garlic, salt, pepper, herbs, chilli and wine.

. Cover and cook on low for 8–9 hours or on high for 6–8 hours. An hour before it's time to eat, use a fork or a pair of tongs to pick out every bone you can find. After you've taken out all the bones, add the beans and chickpeas and put the lid back on until ready to serve.

. Serve with crispy bread.

TANGY VEGAN CORN CHOWDER

SERVES 4

INGREDIENTS

**800 g (1 lb 10 oz) canned whole
 kernel corn**

750 ml (1½ pints) vegetable stock

3 potatoes, diced

1 large onion, diced

1 clove garlic, minced

2 red chilli peppers, minced

1 tablespoon chilli powder

2 teaspoons salt

1 tablespoon dried parsley flakes

**freshly ground black pepper to
 taste**

500 ml (1 pint) soy milk

45 g (1½ oz) margarine

juice of 1 lime

METHOD

. Place the corn, vegetable stock, potatoes, onion, garlic, red chilli peppers, chilli powder, salt, parsley and black pepper to taste in the slow cooker. Cover and cook on low for 7–8 hours.

. Pour the vegetable mixture into a blender, filling the jug no more than halfway. Carefully start the blender using a few quick pulses before leaving it on to purée. Purée in batches until smooth and pour into a clean pot.

. Once everything has been puréed, return it to the slow cooker. Stir the soy milk and margarine into the mixture, cover and cook on low for 1 hour more. Add the lime juice to serve.

LAMB SHANK SOUP

SERVES 8–10

INGREDIENTS

1 tablespoon olive oil

3 lamb shanks

1 large onion, diced

1 sachet vegetable dry soup mix

400 g (14 oz) canned chopped
   tomatoes

2 tablespoons tomato paste

4 tablespoons Worcestershire
   sauce

4 cups diced vegetables (carrots,
   potatoes (scrubbed, skin on),
   parsnips, turnips, corn, celery,
   capsicum (bell pepper)

3 L (6 pints) beef stock

1 tablespoon dried mixed herbs

salt and freshly ground black
   pepper

METHOD

. Heat oil in a large-heavy based frypan. Add shanks and cook over a
   medium heat until browned on each side.

. Put shanks in the slow cooker and add remaining ingredients and
   mix well. Cover and cook on high for 4–6 hours or on low for
   8–10 hours.

. Using a fork, remove meat from bones and coarsely chop or shred.
   Remove bones from soup. Taste and season. If desired, refrigerate
   soup so any fat that sets on the surface can be easily removed. The
   flavor will only improve when the soup is reheated.

CHICKEN NOODLE SOUP

SERVES 4

INGREDIENTS

1 L (2 pints) chicken stock

2 carrots, chopped

2 potatoes, chopped

250 g (8 oz) frozen corn

1 head broccoli, chopped

¼ onion, chopped

2 cloves garlic, minced

salt and freshly ground black
   pepper

2 chicken breasts, chopped

100 g (3½ oz) pasta noodles,
   broken up

METHOD

. Put all ingredients except the chicken and pasta in the slow cooker
   on high for 2 hours. Add the chicken and cook for another hour
   on low, and add the pasta for the last 30 minutes.

POULTRY

THAI GREEN CHICKEN CURRY

SERVES 4

INGREDIENTS

1 kg (2.2 lb) chicken breast, diced

2 tablespoons olive oil

3 tablespoons green curry paste

400 ml (13 fl oz) coconut milk

100 g (3½ oz) green beans, chopped

100 g (3½ oz) cauliflower, chopped

1 red capsicum (bell pepper), chopped

2 teaspoons sugar

METHOD

. In a heavy-based frypan, heat the olive oil and brown the chicken.

. Place all ingredients including the chicken into the slow cooker and combine.

. Cover and cook on high for 6–7 hours or low for 8–10 hours.

. Serve with steamed jasmine rice.

CREAMY CHICKEN CASSEROLE

SERVES 4

INGREDIENTS

1½ kg (3.3 lb) chicken thigh
  fillets, cubed

2 tablespoons plain flour

salt and freshly ground black
  pepper

1 onion, chopped

4 rashers bacon, chopped

125 g (4 oz) mushrooms, chopped

45 g (1½ oz) butter

400 ml (13 fl oz) canned
  mushroom soup

250 ml (8 fl oz) water

60 ml (2 fl oz) thickened cream

fresh parsley, chopped

METHOD

. Coat chicken pieces with flour and season with salt and pepper.

. In a heavy-based frypan, sauté onion, bacon and mushrooms in the butter.

. Place chicken in the slow cooker, add bacon mixture and pour in soup and water (add more water if the sauce is too thick). Stir well. Cover and cook on low for about 6 hours.

. Before serving, stir in cream and garnish with parsley.

AMERICAN CHICKEN CASSEROLE

SERVES 4

INGREDIENTS

2 tablespoons oil

8 chicken drumsticks

salt and freshly ground black pepper

4 onions, sliced

300 ml (10 fl oz) chicken stock

½ teaspoon chilli powder

2 tablespoons plain flour

2 x 400 g (14 oz) canned tomatoes

1 x 400 g (14 oz) canned red kidney beans, rinsed, drained

50 g (1½ oz) butter

METHOD

. Heat the oil in a large frypan over medium heat. Add the chicken, season and cook until browned.

. Add the onions and fry for 1 minute.

. Heat stock in a small saucepan until simmering.

. In a preheated slow cooker set on high, sprinkle the chilli powder and flour. Slowly add the stock, stirring constantly. Transfer chicken and onions to the slow cooker and add the tomatoes, beans and butter. Cover and cook for 3½ hours on high.

CHICKEN MANDARIN

SERVES 4

INGREDIENTS

3 white onions, sliced

1 clove garlic, crushed

2 carrots, diced

4 large chicken breast fillets

salt and seasoned pepper blend

400 g (14 oz) canned mandarins in syrup

1 tablespoon honey

2 teaspoons Angostura bitters

100 g (3½ oz) French onion soup mix

zest of ½ orange, julienned

METHOD

. Place onion, garlic and carrots in slow cooker. Coat chicken breasts evenly with mixed salt and pepper blend and place on top of vegetables.

. Mix together the mandarin syrup, honey and bitters, then stir in the soup mix and pour into slow cooker. Cook on low for 6–8 hours. After 3 hours, add mandarin segments and orange zest.

. Remove chicken when cooked. If liquid looks too thin, reduce on a high heat or thicken with 2 tablespoons cornflour (cornstarch).

. Serve on rice, and garnish with chopped parsley.

SLOW-ROAST CHICKEN

SERVES 4

INGREDIENTS

**1 whole chicken, about 1¼ kg
(2½ lb)**

1 sachet of French onion soup

2 red onions, cut into chunks

2 cloves garlic, sliced

125 ml (4 fl oz) white wine

METHOD

. Wash the chicken and pat dry. Sprinkle the French onion soup mix over the chicken and rub in.

. Scatter the onions and garlic over the bottom of the slow cooker and place the chicken on top.

. Cover and cook on low for 6–8 hours.

CHICKEN CRÊPES

SERVES 6–8 (ABOUT 16 CRÊPES)

INGREDIENTS

1½ kg (3 lb) roasting chicken

2 chicken stock cubes, crumbled

1 onion, chopped

3 sprigs parsley

1 sprig thyme

120 g (4 oz) butter

1 spring onion (scallion), finely
   chopped

600 g (21 oz) button mushrooms,
   sliced

4 tablespoons plain (all-purpose)
   flour

salt and freshly ground black
   pepper

375 ml (12 fl oz) milk

1 tablespoon dry sherry

2 tablespoons thickened cream

3 hard-boiled eggs, chopped

CRÊPE BATTER

2 cups plain (all-purpose) flour

pinch of salt

2 eggs, beaten

1 tablespoon olive oil

500 ml (1 pint) milk

METHOD

. Place chicken in slow cooker, add stock cubes, onion and herbs
and cover with water. Cook on low for 4–5 hours or high for 3–4
hours. Remove chicken and chop flesh finely, discarding skin and
bones. Reserve ½ cup stock. Melt butter in frying pan and sauté
spring onion and mushrooms until softened but not brown. Blend
in flour, season and cook for 1 minute.

. Combine the milk and reserved stock and add to the pan gradually,
stirring. Add sherry and cream, then cook gently until stock
thickens. Adjust seasoning if necessary and fold through cooked
chicken and hard-boiled eggs. Keep mixture warm in slow cooker
on high, with lid slightly ajar.

. To make batter, sift the flour and salt together and make a well in
the centre. Add the eggs, oil, and one cup of milk. Beat gradually
drawing in flour from the sides. Slowly add remaining milk and
4 tablespoons water, making a thin batter. Cover and set aside for
at least an hour. Heat a little butter in a heavy-based 15 cm (6 in)
frying pan. Add a little batter and tilt pan so that batter spreads
evenly. When cooked on one side, turn and cook other side. Pile
crêpes in a tea towel and keep warm.

. Preheat the oven to 180°C (360°F). Place a spoonful of chicken
sauce onto each crêpe, roll up and place into a greased ovenproof
dish. Spoon over some of the sauce and bake for about 10 minutes.
Serve remainder of sauce in a small jug at the table.

CITRUS CHICKEN

SERVES 4–5

INGREDIENTS

1 lemon

1½ kg (3 lb) roasting chicken

1 bouquet garni

3 carrots, thinly sliced

6 onions, thinly sliced

125 ml (4 fl oz) chicken stock

salt and freshly ground black
   pepper

pinch of nutmeg

1 tablespoon toasted flaked
   almonds

¼ cup parsley, chopped

CREAM SAUCE

125 ml (4 fl oz) thin cream

175 g (6 oz) button mushrooms,
   sliced

METHOD

. Halve the lemon, squeeze out the juice and brush it all over the chicken. Place lemon skins in the chicken cavity.

. Lightly grease the slow cooker and add the bouquet garni. Place the chicken on top and arrange the carrot and onion around the outside. Pour around the stock, season to taste, add nutmeg, then cook for approximately 6 hours on low or 4–5 hours on high (cooking time will vary depending on the tenderness of the chicken).

. To make the sauce, saute the mushrooms. Remove about ½ cup of chicken stock from the slow cooker, skim off as much fat as possible, and bring to the boil in a small saucepan. Add the stock and reduce, then add the cream and reduce to make a pouring sauce.

. Serve chicken with the cream sauce.

MUSTARD CHICKEN

SERVES 3–4

INGREDIENTS

3 carrots, peeled and diced

3 large onions, finely chopped

1 clove garlic, crushed

2 teaspoons dried thyme

1 bay leaf

salt and seasoned pepper blend

500 g (1 lb) lean pork, skinned
    and sliced

1½ kg (3 lb) chicken, jointed

4 rashers bacon, rinds removed

125 ml (4 fl oz) dry white wine

60 ml (2 fl oz) brandy

MUSTARD SAUCE

1 egg yolk

3 tablespoons thickened cream

1 tablespoon Dijon mustard

METHOD

. In a bowl, combine the carrot, onion, garlic, herbs and salt and
pepper. Place half the pork in the base of the slow cooker, then
add half the vegetables. Add the chicken pieces, the remaining
vegetables, then the remaining pork. Place bacon rashers on top.

. Pour over combined wine and brandy. Place a piece of foil over
the slow cooker, then cover with lid and cook on low for around
5 hours (cooking time may vary depending on the tenderness of
the chicken).

. To make the sauce, drain off the cooking liquid, skim off any
fat and pour into a small saucepan. Beat egg yolk and cream
together, add to saucepan and whisk. Cook gently until thick,
but do not allow to boil. Add the mustard and whisk until
thoroughly blended.

. Arrange chicken pieces, pork and vegetables on warmed serving
platter, and pour over the mustard sauce. Serve with potatoes,
sprinkled with parsley.

Note: Rabbit can be used in this recipe instead of chicken.

LEMONGRASS
AND GINGER-SCENTED CHICKEN

SERVES 4–6

INGREDIENTS

2 kg (4.4 lb) skinless chicken thigh fillets

2 medium onions, sliced

3 cloves garlic, crushed

5 cm (2 in) piece ginger, peeled and sliced

2 large red chillies, deseeded and sliced

2 stalks lemongrass, bruised

125 ml (4 fl oz) chicken stock

60 ml (2 fl oz) soy sauce

2 tablespoons oyster sauce

freshly ground black pepper

200 g (7 oz) sugar snap peas

METHOD

.   In a heavy-based frypan, heat oil and quickly seal sides of chicken in batches. Transfer to slow cooker.

.   Reduce heat, add onions and garlic to the same pan and sauté for 1–2 minutes. Place in slow cooker with remaining ingredients except the sugar snap peas.

.   Cover and cook on high for 3–4 hours or low for 5–6 hours.

.   About 15 minutes before serving, add sugar snap peas and stir through. Remove lemongrass before serving.

ITALIAN CHICKEN AND POTATOES

SERVES 2

INGREDIENTS

2 skinless chicken breast fillets

125 ml (4 fl oz) Italian salad dressing

1 teaspoon Italian seasoning

40 g (1½ oz) Parmesan or Romano cheese, grated

4 potatoes, peeled and cut into wedges

METHOD

. Place chicken in bottom of slow cooker. Sprinkle with half of the Italian dressing, seasoning and grated cheese. Put the potatoes on top or around the chicken. Sprinkle with the rest of the dressing, seasoning and cheese. Cook on low for 6–8 hours.

. This simple and delicious recipe is perfect with a simple tossed salad.

LEMON GARLIC CHICKEN

SERVES 4

INGREDIENTS

4 skinless chicken breast fillets

2 teaspoons dried oregano

1 teaspoon sea salt

1 teaspoon freshly ground black
  pepper

1 tablespoon cornflour

2 tablespoons oil

250 ml (8 fl oz) chicken stock

4 tablespoons fresh lemon juice

125 ml (4 fl oz) white wine

4 cloves garlic, crushed

125 ml (4 fl oz) cream

METHOD

. Wash chicken and dry with absorbent paper.

. Combine oregano, salt, pepper and cornflour in a small bowl.
  Sprinkle on the chicken and rub it in.

. In a heavy-based frypan fry the chicken breasts in the olive oil until
  browned. Transfer the browned chicken to the slow cooker.

. Combine the stock, lemon juice, wine and garlic and add to the
  slow cooker. Cover and cook on high for 3–4 hours or on low for
  6–7 hours.

. Remove chicken to serving plates and keep warm. Add cream to
  the remaining liquid and stir well and heat in a small pan to serve
  over the chicken.

PORTUGUESE JUGGED CHICKEN

SERVES 4

INGREDIENTS

60 g (2 oz) butter

8 small onions, peeled

1.5 kg (3.3 lb) whole chicken

3 tomatoes, cut into wedges

**100 g (3½ oz) smoked ham or
    bacon, diced**

2 bay leaves

2 cloves garlic, crushed

2 teaspoons Dijon mustard

180 ml (6 fl oz) dry white wine

60 ml (2 fl oz) port wine

2 tablespoons brandy

**salt and freshly ground black
    pepper**

METHOD

.   Melt 20 g (¾ oz) butter in a large heavy-based frypan over medium heat. Add onions and cook for 2 minutes, stirring constantly. Brush chicken all over with the remaining butter. Add chicken to pan and cook for 4 minutes.

.   In a slow cooker set on low, arrange tomatoes, ham or bacon and bay leaves over base of dish. Add the contents of the frypan and splash the pan with a little of the white wine and add to the slow cooker as well.

.   Blend together garlic, mustard, remaining white wine, port wine, brandy, salt and pepper. Pour over chicken, cover and cook for 7 hours.

.   As an alternative you can carefully remove the ceramic insert with the jugged chicken in the last 15 minutes of cooking and put it in an oven preheated to 200°C. Bake with the lid removed to brown the chicken. Cut the chicken into pieces and serve with crispy potatoes and salad.

APRICOT CHICKEN

SERVES 4

INGREDIENTS

400 ml (13 fl oz) apricot nectar

1 sachet French onion soup

1 tablespoon curry powder

400 g (14 oz) canned apricots, drained

600 g (1 lb 5 oz) chicken breasts or thigh fillets

METHOD

. Cut the chicken into small pieces. Place all ingredients into the slow cooker and stir until well mixed.

. Cover and cook on low for around 8 hours.

. Serve with steamed rice and vegetables or pasta.

Note: This family favorite of succulent chicken and juicy apricots delivers full, rich flavors every time.

BURGUNDY CHICKEN CASSEROLE

SERVES 4–6

INGREDIENTS

8 skinless chicken thigh fillets

salt and freshly ground black pepper, to taste

1 onion, sliced

100 g (3½ oz) brown mushrooms, sliced

1 red capsicum (bell pepper), sliced

1 sachet spicy tomato and onion soup

375 ml (12 fl oz) chicken stock

250 ml (8 fl oz) red wine

1 tablespoon tomato paste

1 teaspoon Worcestershire sauce

1 teaspoon dried thyme

METHOD

. Place chicken in slow cooker. Season and cover with onion, mushroom and red capsicum. Combine remaining ingredients and pour over chicken and vegetables.

. Cover and cook for about 6–7 hours on low. Remove chicken and stir sauce before serving.

TURKEY PÂTÉ

INGREDIENTS

1 kg (2 lb) frozen turkey
   hindquarter

3 chicken stock cubes, crumbled

1 onion, sliced

1 stalk celery with leaves, sliced

1 carrot, roughly diced

salt and freshly ground black
   pepper

2 tablespoons chopped liverwurst
   sausage

1 teaspoon dried thyme

4 spring onions (scallions), finely
   chopped

¼ cup parsley, chopped

125 ml (4 fl oz) thin cream

2 tablespoons coleslaw dressing

METHOD

. Thaw turkey hindquarter and remove as much fat and skin as possible, then place into slow cooker with stock cubes, onion, celery, carrot and salt and pepper to taste.

. Cook on low for approximately 5–6 hours or on high for 4–5 hours. Test for tenderness. When cooked, remove turkey, carefully wipe off any residual fat and allow to cool. Remove as much turkey meat as possible from the bones, then dice.

. Using a food processor or blender, combine diced turkey meat, liverwurst, thyme, onions, parsley and a little of the cream.

. Combine remaining cream with dressing and pour in, blending until quite smooth. Add salt and pepper to taste.

. Serve in small pots, accompanied by very lightly buttered wholemeal bread.

FRICASSÉED CHICKEN WITH VINEGAR

SERVES 4

INGREDIENTS

60 ml (2 fl oz) olive oil

1 kg (2 lb) chicken thigh fillets, quartered

freshly ground black pepper

2 large cloves garlic, chopped

2 sprigs fresh rosemary, leaves removed and chopped

5 anchovy fillets, chopped

125 ml (4 fl oz) white wine vinegar

2 tablespoons balsamic vinegar

20 Kalamata olives

METHOD

. In a heavy-based frying pan, heat the olive oil and brown the chicken pieces all over, seasoning well with pepper. Transfer to a plate and keep warm. Turn the heat to low and add garlic, rosemary and anchovies. Stir until the mixture is aromatic.

. Transfer the garlic mixture and chicken to the slow cooker. Add the white wine vinegar and cook on high for about 1½ hours or until the chicken is tender. Just before serving, stir in the balsamic vinegar and olives.

. This dish is delicious served with spinach and potatoes roasted in olive oil and rosemary.

DUCK BRAISED IN BRANDY AND PORT

SERVES 4

INGREDIENTS

1 kg (2 lb) plump duck

4 tablespoons plain (all-purpose) flour

60 g (2 oz) butter

2 tablespoons olive oil

2 rashers bacon, chopped

1 large onion, chopped

60 g (2 oz) small mushrooms, sliced

4 tablespoons brandy

4 tablespoons port

salt and freshly ground black pepper

½ teaspoon dried thyme

METHOD

. Pat duck dry with absorbent paper, and rub lightly with 2 tablespoons flour.

. Heat butter and oil in a frying pan and brown duck on all sides. Remove and place in slow cooker.

. Add a little extra butter to frying pan if necessary, then add bacon, onion and mushrooms. Sauté until golden brown. Pour half the brandy and half the port into the pan and simmer for 1–2 minutes. Add remaining flour and cook until very well browned.

. Gradually add 1 cup water, stirring constantly. Season to taste, add thyme and spoon sauce over duck in slow cooker. Cook for approximately 5 hours on low. About 30 minutes before serving, stir remaining port and brandy into sauce around duck.

. Serve with green vegetables.

MOROCCAN-STYLE CHICKEN WINGS

SERVES 6

INGREDIENTS

2 tablespoons vegetable oil

1 kg (2 lb) chicken wings

1 large onion, finely chopped

1 clove garlic, crushed

2 cm (¾ in) piece ginger, grated

½ teaspoon ground turmeric

½ teaspoon ground cumin

1 cinnamon stick

60 ml (2 fl oz) cider vinegar

500 ml (1 pint) apricot nectar

salt and freshly ground black
    pepper

90 g (3 oz) pitted prunes, pitted

90 g (3 oz) dried apricots

1 tablespoon honey

60 ml (2 fl oz) lemon juice

fresh parsley, chopped

METHOD

. Heat the oil in a large saucepan and brown the chicken wings in batches. Remove browned wings to a plate. Add the onion to the pan and cook for 2 minutes. Stir in the garlic and cook for a further minute.

. Transfer the onion and garlic to the slow cooker. Add the chicken, ginger and spices, and stir to coat wings with spices. Add the vinegar and apricot nectar, season to taste and cook on low for 6 hours.

. Add the prunes, apricots, honey and lemon juice to the cooker and simmer for 2 more hours. Remove lid, turn to high and simmer for 35 minutes. If a thicker sauce is desired, remove the wings and fruit to a serving platter and simmer until the sauce reduces and thickens.

. Serve wings immediately on a bed of steamed couscous and pour over the sauce. Garnish with parsley.

GINGER CHICKEN AND PINEAPPLE SALAD

SERVES 6

INGREDIENTS

1½ kg (3 lb) roasting chicken

salt and peppercorns

2 cloves garlic

2 small white onions, sliced into
   rings

30 g (1 oz) ginger, grated

1 pineapple, cubed

1 red capsicum (bell pepper)

2 tablespoons vinaigrette or
   coleslaw dressing

fresh parsley, chopped

METHOD

. Place the chicken in the slow cooker and cover with cold water. Add the salt, peppercorns, garlic and half the onion and ginger and cook on low for approximately 5 hours or on high for 3 hours (cooking time will vary depending on the tenderness of the chicken—the flesh should not be falling off the bones). Remove chicken from stock and allow to cool. Retain stock for soups.

. Shred chicken into bite-size pieces. Combine with remaining onion and ginger and all other ingredients except dressing and parsley. Toss salad with dressing and garnish with parsley.

LAMB

LAMB HOTPOT WITH POTATO DUMPLINGS

SERVES 4

INGREDIENTS

2 tablespoons plain flour

1 kg (2.2 lb) diced lamb

60 ml (2 fl oz) olive oil

4 rashers rindless bacon, chopped

1 large brown onion, finely
   chopped

2 cloves garlic, crushed

2 tablespoons tomato paste

400 g (14 oz) canned diced
   tomatoes

250 ml (8 fl oz) beef stock

2 cups mixed frozen vegetables

POTATO DUMPLINGS

350 g (12 oz) desiree potatoes, cut
   into large pieces

50 g (1¾ oz) butter, chopped

150 ml (5 fl oz) milk

1¼ cups self-raising flour, sifted

100 g (3½ oz) aged Cheddar
   cheese, grated

60 g (2 oz) flat-leaf parsley,
   chopped

METHOD

. To make the dumplings, steam the potatoes for 10 minutes or until just tender.

. Transfer to a bowl, add butter and mash roughly. Add milk, flour, cheese and parsley and stir with a wooden spoon until smooth. Divide mixture into 12 portions and roll each portion into a ball.

. To make hotpot, place all ingredients in the slow cooker. Cover and cook on low for 4–5 hours.

. Meanwhile, preheat the oven to 200°C (400°F). When hotpot is cooked, remove ceramic dish from slow cooker, place dumplings in a single layer on top, transfer to the oven and bake uncovered for 25–30 minutes until dumplings are golden.

LAMB ROAST

SERVES 6

INGREDIENTS

2 tablespoons tomato pasta sauce
1 tablespoon fruit chutney
1 teaspoon curry powder
6 cloves garlic, crushed
1 leg of lamb
2 tablespoons olive oil

METHOD

. Mix pasta sauce, chutney, curry powder and garlic together and set aside.

. In a heavy-based frypan, brown the lamb in the olive oil. Place lamb in the slow cooker and pour the tomato mixture over the lamb.

. Cover and cook on low for 6–7 hours or on high for 4–5 hours.

. Serve with roast vegetables.

LAMB BALLS

SERVES 4

INGREDIENTS

750 g (1 lb 8 oz) lean minced lamb

½ cup cold mashed potatoes

1 egg

⅓ cup pine nuts

3 tablespoons dried currants

¼ cup fresh parsley, very finely chopped

¼ teaspoon ground allspice

2 cloves garlic, minced

salt and freshly ground black pepper

1 teaspoon vegetable oil

1 medium onion, chopped

250 ml (8 fl oz) tomato pasta sauce

60 ml (2 fl oz) dry red wine

METHOD

. Mix lamb, potatoes, egg, nuts, currants, parsley, allspice, garlic, salt and pepper together well. Shape into balls.

. Heat oil in a large heavy-based frypan. Brown meatballs on all sides and transfer to the slow cooker.

. Add onion to frypan and sauté until limp and glazed. Add tomato sauce and wine. Bring to the boil and pour over meatballs.

. Cover and cook on low for 1½–2 hours.

LAMB CURRY

SERVES 6

INGREDIENTS

1 kg (2.2 lb) boneless lamb

2 tablespoons curry powder

1 tablespoon olive oil

2 apples, peeled and diced

2 onions, chopped

2 cm (¾ in) fresh ginger, minced

2 tablespoons plain flour

2 cloves garlic, minced

250 ml (8 fl oz) dry red wine

250 ml (8 fl oz) beef stock

1 teaspoon lemon juice

salt and freshly ground black
    pepper

fresh parsley, chopped

METHOD

. In a large heavy-based frypan, brown meat and curry powder in olive oil. Transfer to the slow cooker.

. Add apples, onions, ginger and flour to frypan and cook until glazed. Transfer to slow cooker.

. Add garlic, wine, stock, lemon juice, salt and pepper and mix well. Cover and cook on low for 8–10 hours.

. Serve over steamed rice and garnish with parsley.

LAMB BOULANGÈRE

SERVES 4–5

INGREDIENTS

2 white onions, thinly sliced
2 potatoes, thinly sliced
2 tomatoes, peeled and sliced
salt and freshly ground black
pepper
½ bunch thyme
1 clove garlic, quartered
1 small leg of lamb, trimmed of
fat and gristle
125 ml (4 fl oz) beef stock

METHOD

. Layer vegetables in slow cooker, seasoning and adding thyme
sprigs between layers.

. Rub cut surfaces of garlic well over lamb, then season and
place on vegetable bed. Pour in stock and cook on low for
approximately 8–10 hours. Skim as much fat as possible from
surface of liquid and serve lamb in thick slices, with vegetables
and juices spooned over.

. If preferred, lamb may be browned in a hot oven just before
serving.

LANCASHIRE HOTPOT

SERVES 4–6

INGREDIENTS

8 forequarter, neck or chump
   lamb chops, trimmed of fat
6 carrots, peeled and thinly sliced
6 parsnips, peeled and thinly
   sliced
6 onions, peeled and thinly sliced
6 potatoes, peeled, parboiled and
   sliced
salt and freshly ground black
   pepper
fresh parsley, chopped

METHOD

. Layer all ingredients except parsley in the slow cooker, ending with
   a layer of potatoes. Cover with water and cook on low for 8 hours
   or overnight, until lamb is falling off bones. Skim off any fat.

. To serve, ladle out the meat and vegetables, spoon over the
   flavorsome juices and sprinkle with parsley.

. This dish is wonderful with crusty bread to mop up the juices.

IRISH STEW

SERVES 4

INGREDIENTS

2 large onions, sliced

1 kg (2.2 lb) lamb neck pieces

2 teaspoons mixed dried herbs

salt and freshly ground black
   pepper

2–3 large potatoes, peeled, sliced

500 ml (1½ pints) chicken stock

1 tablespoon chopped fresh
   parsley to garnish

METHOD

. Place one quarter of the onions in a slow cooker and place the lamb on top. Sprinkle with herbs and season well.

. Combine remaining onions and potatoes and place over lamb. Season well, pour over stock and cook for 5½ hours on high.

. Serve sprinkled with freshly chopped parsley and steamed vegetables.

HERB AND GARLIC LAMB SHANKS

SERVES 4

INGREDIENTS

4 meaty lamb shanks

2 cloves garlic, crushed

1 tablespoon dijon mustard

2 tablespoons olive oil

750 ml (1½ pints) chicken stock

2 teaspoons dried rosemary

2 teaspoons dried Italian herbs

**salt and freshly ground black
    pepper**

METHOD

. Score the outside of the lamb shanks and rub crushed garlic and
  Dijon mustard into them.

. In a heavy-based frypan, heat the olive oil and brown the lamb
  shanks.

. Place the browned lamb in the slow cooker, then pour in the
  chicken stock and sprinkle the herbs over the lamb. Add salt and
  freshly ground black pepper to taste.

. Cook on low for 8–9 hours or 4–5 hours on high.

BURGUNDY LAMB SHANKS

SERVES 4

INGREDIENTS

2 kg (4.4 lb) lamb shanks
salt and freshly ground black
   pepper
grated zest of ½ lemon
½ teaspoon dried oregano
2 cloves garlic, minced
¼ cup fresh parsley, chopped
1 carrot, peeled and chopped
1 onion, chopped
1 teaspoon olive oil
250 ml (8 oz) dry red wine
1 beef stock cube, crumbled

METHOD

. Season shanks with salt, pepper, lemon zest and oregano. Place in the slow cooker and sprinkle with garlic and parsley.

. In a heavy-based frypan, sauté carrot and onion in oil and transfer to slow cooker. Pour wine into frypan and add stock cube. Deglaze frypan and stir juices into slow cooker.

. Cover and cook on low for 8 hours. If you wish to have a thicker sauce, drain cooking liquid into a saucepan and boil to reduce and thicken slightly.

SLOW-SIMMERED LAMB SHANKS WITH COUSCOUS

SERVES 4

INGREDIENTS

4 lamb shanks, French cut*

300 g (10 oz) canned chopped tomatoes

250 ml (8 fl oz) dry red wine

1 bay leaf

6 sprigs fresh thyme

1 cinnamon stick

200 g (7 oz) butternut pumpkin, chopped

2 zucchini (courgettes), chopped

8 dried apricots

8 dried prunes

1 cup couscous

500 ml (1 pint) boiling water

2 tablespoons flaked almonds, toasted

METHOD

. Heat a large frypan over a high heat and add lamb and cook until browned. Transfer to a slow cooker set on high.

. Add the tomatoes, wine, bay leaf, thyme and cinnamon stick. Cover and cook for 3 hours.

. Add the pumpkin, zucchini, apricots and prunes and cook for a further 2 hours on a low setting or until the vegetables are soft and the lamb starts to come away from the bone.

. Meanwhile, put the couscous in a large bowl, cover with boiling water and allow to stand for 10 minutes or until all the liquid is absorbed.

. Serve the lamb shanks on top of the couscous, garnished with the flaked almonds.

Note: The term French cut (or Frenched) refers to the cutting and scraping of all meat, fat and gristle from the shank, leaving the meaty part virtually fat-free.

LAMB AND EGGPLANT CASSEROLE

SERVES 4

INGREDIENTS

1 tablespoon olive oil

1 small eggplant (aubergine),
   sliced

250 g (8 oz) minced lamb

3 large ripe tomatoes, peeled and
   sliced

salt and freshly ground black
   pepper

6 fresh basil leaves, finely
   shredded

120 g (4 oz) Swiss cheese, grated

METHOD

. Heat the oil in a large frying pan over medium heat. Add eggplant
  and cook until golden brown. Drain on absorbent paper.

. Add the minced lamb and cook for 3–4 minutes or until browned.
  Drain off any excess fat.

. In a small casserole dish that fits into your slow cooker, arrange a
  layer of eggplant slices, a layer of minced lamb and a layer of sliced
  tomato, and sprinkle with salt and pepper and half of the basil.
  Cover with grated cheese. Repeat layers until casserole dish is filled,
  ending with a cheese layer.

. Place casserole in slow cooker and cook on high for approximately
  2 hours.

. If preferred, casserole may be placed under griller (broiler) for a
  minute or two to brown the cheese topping before serving.

BEEF

BEEF EN DAUBE

SERVES 6

INGREDIENTS

2 rashers bacon, diced

1 kg (2.2 lb) lean stewing beef, cut
into 25 mm (1 in) cubes

2 cloves garlic, minced

24 small pickling onions

2 tablespoons olive oil

1 tablespoon red wine vinegar

1 tablespoon brown sugar, firmly
packed

375 ml (12 fl oz) dry red wine

salt and freshly ground black
pepper

½ teaspoon dried thyme

250 ml (8 fl oz) beef stock

2 strips orange zest

2 tablespoons cornflour

fresh parsley, chopped

METHOD

. In a large heavy-based frypan, sauté bacon until crisp. Remove
from frypan and set aside.

. Brown meat, garlic and onions in olive oil and transfer to the slow
cooker with bacon.

. Add vinegar and brown sugar to frypan. Cook for 1 minute,
stirring. Pour in wine and bring to the boil, season and pour over
the meat. Then add the dried thyme, stock and orange zest to the
slow cooker. Cook on low for 8 hours.

. Turn slow cooker to high. When bubbling, mix cornflour with
2 tablespoons water and stir in. Cook, stirring, until thickened.
Garnish with parsley and serve.

BEEF CARBONADE

SERVES 4

INGREDIENTS

2 tablespoons vegetable oil

1 kg (2.2 lb) gravy beef, cut into 2
cm (¾ in) cubes

1 large onion, thinly sliced

1 tablespoon plain flour

2 tablespoons brown sugar

375 ml (12 fl oz) stout

500 ml (1 pint) beef stock

1 tablespoon tomato paste

1 bouquet garni

salt and freshly ground black
pepper

chopped fresh parsley to garnish

METHOD

. Heat the oil in a large frypan over medium heat. Add one-third of
the beef and cook until browned. Remove from the pan while you
cook the remaining batches, adding more oil if necessary. Set the
beef aside.

. Lower the heat, add the onion and cook for 5 minutes, stirring.
Sprinkle in the flour and sugar and stir for 1–2 minutes, then add
½ cup of the stout and swirl to collect all of the flavor from the
pan. Pour into a slow cooker set on low. Add the remaining stout,
stock, sautéed beef, tomato paste and bouquet garni. Season and
stir well, then cover.

. Cook for 10 hours. Stir 2–3 times during cooking, adding a little
water if necessary. Discard the bouquet garni and season again if
necessary.

BOEUF À LA MODE

SERVES 10

INGREDIENTS

2 kg (4.4 lb) beef rump roast
1 teaspoon olive oil
1 teaspoon sesame oil
500 ml (1 pint) beef stock
60 ml (2 fl oz) tomato sauce

MARINADE

½ teaspoon salt
½ teaspoon dried thyme
freshly ground black pepper
1 carrot, peeled and chopped
1 stalk celery, chopped
1 onion, chopped
2 cloves garlic, minced
500 ml (1 pint) dry red wine

METHOD

. To make the marinade, combine ingredients in a large bowl.

. Place roast in a large bowl with the marinade. Cover and marinate for 1 day in the refrigerator. Turn occasionally.

. To cook, remove meat from marinade and pat dry with absorbent paper. Heat oils in a large heavy-based frypan and brown meat on all sides.

. Transfer meat to the slow cooker. Strain marinade, reserving vegetables and add marinade to meat. Sauté vegetables in frypan until glazed then add to meat. Deglaze pan with 1 cup water and add to slow cooker with beef stock and tomato sauce.

. Cover and cook on low for 8 hours, or until meat is tender. Transfer meat to a carving board. Pour juices into a saucepan and boil until reduced. Pour juices into a sauce boat, garnish with chopped parsley and serve with the meat.

FAMILY MEAT BALLS

SERVES 4–6

INGREDIENTS

2 teaspoons olive oil

1 medium onion, finely chopped

500 g (1.1 lb) lean beef mince

500 g (1.1 lb) minced turkey meat

**salt and freshly ground black
    pepper**

teaspoon dried tarragon

¼ teaspoon dried basil

2 tablespoons plain flour

60 ml (2 fl oz) tomato paste

180 ml (6 fl oz) beef stock

2 teaspoons Worcestershire sauce

2 teaspoons apple cider vinegar

250 g (8 oz) mushrooms, sliced

250 ml (8 oz) sour cream

METHOD

. Heat 1 teaspoon olive oil in a large heavy-based frypan. Sauté onion until golden and transfer to the slow cooker.

. Shape meat into bite-size balls. Drop into frypan and sauté, shaking to turn, until browned. Sprinkle with salt, pepper, tarragon, basil and flour. Cook for a few minutes, then transfer to slow cooker.

. Add tomato paste, beef stock, Worcestershire sauce and vinegar to frying pan. Stir to deglaze pan. Pour into slow cooker, cover and cook on high for 1½–2 hours.

. Sauté mushrooms in remaining olive oil. Add to slow cooker along with sour cream. Heat thoroughly, then serve with French bread.

MEDITERRANEAN BEEF STEW

SERVES 6

INGREDIENTS

2 tablespoons oil

1 kg (2.2 lb) lean stewing beef,
   trimmed, cut into large cubes

2 onions, sliced

2 cloves garlic, chopped

1 eggplant (aubergine), diced

250 ml (8 fl oz) beef stock

400 g (14 oz) canned whole
   peeled tomatoes, chopped

¼ cup tapioca

1 teaspoon ground cinnamon

1 bay leaf

2 teaspoons salt

freshly ground black pepper

400 g (14 oz) canned chickpeas,
   rinsed, drained

fresh oregano leaves to garnish

METHOD

. Heat the oil in a large frypan over a medium heat. Add meat and cook for 5 minutes, turning occasionally. Add the onions and garlic and cook for a further 5 minutes, stirring constantly. Drain off any excess fats. Place the beef mixture and eggplant in a slow cooker.

. Combine stock with juice from canned tomatoes, tapioca, cinnamon, bay leaf, salt and pepper and pour into slow cooker; stir well. Cover and cook on low setting for 8 hours.

. Approximately 30 minutes before serving turn to high, stir in chickpeas and tomatoes and cook for the remaining time.

. Serve garnished with fresh oregano leaves.

SAVORY STEAK

SERVES 6

INGREDIENTS

750 g (1 lb 8 oz) round steak
¼ cup plain flour
2 teaspoons mustard powder
**salt and freshly ground black
  pepper**
1 teaspoon olive oil
1 onion, finely chopped
2 carrots, peeled and grated
2 stalks celery, finely chopped
400 g (14 oz) canned tomatoes
**2 tablespoons Worcestershire
  sauce**
**2 teaspoons brown sugar, firmly
  packed**
fresh parsley, chopped

METHOD

. Cut steak into 6 serving-size pieces. Coat with mixture of flour, mustard, salt and pepper.

. In a large heavy-based frypan, brown meat in oil. Transfer to the slow cooker.

. In the same frypan, sauté onion, carrots and celery until glazed. Add tomatoes, Worcestershire sauce and brown sugar. Use the mixture to deglaze the pan then pour juices over meat.

. Cover and cook on low for 6–8 hours, or until tender. To serve, spoon sauce over meat and sprinkle with parsley.

POT ROAST

SERVES 8

INGREDIENTS

2 kg (4.4 lb) chuck steak roast

1 tablespoon olive oil

4 cloves garlic, minced

250 ml (8 fl oz) dry sherry

90 ml (3 fl oz) soy sauce

1½ teaspoons ground ginger

freshly ground black pepper

**2 spring onions (scallions), thinly
  sliced**

4 whole cloves

METHOD

. Rub roast with oil and minced garlic. Place meat in a glass or ceramic bowl. Add sherry, soy sauce, ginger, pepper, spring onions and cloves. Turn meat to coat. Cover and refrigerate overnight.

. To cook, remove meat from marinade and set marinade aside. Transfer meat to the slow cooker. Add ½ cup of the reserved marinade. Cover and cook on low for 7–8 hours, or until tender.

. Transfer to a platter and keep warm. Add ½ cup more marinade to pan juices. Cook down until reduced and pour into a sauce boat. Serve sauce with meat.

FRUITY BEEF CURRY

SERVES 4

INGREDIENTS

500 g (1 lb) beef, cubed

1 large cooking apple, peeled and diced

120 g (4 oz) dried apricots, chopped

¼ cup sultanas (golden raisins) or currants

1 strip orange zest

salt and freshly ground black pepper

1 cm (½ in) piece ginger, grated

1 tablespoon lemon juice

½ clove garlic, crushed

250 ml (8 fl oz) beef stock

1–2 tablespoons curry powder

2 tablespoons natural yoghurt

METHOD

. Place beef in slow cooker with apple, apricots, sultanas (golden raisins) or currants, orange zest, salt and pepper to taste, ginger, lemon juice and garlic.

. Blend stock with curry powder, add to cooker and stir gently. Cook on low for approximately 6–8 hours or on high for 5–6 hours (time will vary depending on the meat). About 30 minutes before serving, stir in yoghurt and heat through. Serve with rice and chutney.

. If preferred, beef may be browned first in a frying pan in a little oil. This improves the flavor and color of the dish, but is not essential.

LASAGNE

SERVES 4–6

INGREDIENTS

2 tablespoons olive oil

500 ml (1 pint) water

250 g (8 oz) minced beef

½ teaspoon salt

250 g (8 oz) lean pork, minced

½ teaspoon freshly ground black pepper

1 onion, finely chopped

250 g (8 oz) lasagne sheets

1 clove garlic, finely chopped

30 g (1 oz) mozzarella cheese, sliced thinly

1 teaspoon parsley, chopped

250 g (8 oz) ricotta cheese, crumbed

250 g (8 oz) tomato paste

2 tablespoons Romano cheese, grated

1½ teaspoon salt

METHOD

. Heat oil in a large saucepan, add beef and pork and brown with onion, garlic and parsley.

. Stir in tomato paste, water, ½ teaspoon salt, and pepper and simmer, uncovered, for 1½ hours.

. Preheat oven to 180°C (350°F). Bring a large pot of water to the boil, add the salt and lasagne sheets. Boil for 20 minutes or until al dente, stirring constantly but very gently to prevent lasagne sheets from sticking together. Drain and set aside.

. Wipe a little oil over the base of a large shallow rectangular baking dish, and arrange alternate layers of lasagne sheets, meat sauce, mozzarella and ricotta cheese. Repeat layers until lasagne sheets and sauce and two cheeses are all used, ending with ricotta cheese.

. Sprinkle with grated Romano cheese and bake in the oven for 25–30 minutes. Allow to stand for 10 minutes before serving.

SHORT RIBS

SERVES 4

INGREDIENTS

2 kg (4.4 lb) beef short ribs, cut into 5 cm (2 in) lengths

1 onion, chopped

1 teaspoon olive oil

150 ml (5 fl oz) tomato sauce

3 tablespoons soy sauce

2 tablespoons apple cider vinegar

2 tablespoons brown sugar, firmly packed

METHOD

. Place short ribs on a griller pan and grill until well browned to remove excess fat.

. Transfer to the slow cooker. Sauté onion in oil until limp and golden. Add tomato sauce, soy sauce, vinegar and brown sugar and heat until blended. Pour over ribs.

. Cover and cook on low for 8 hours.

BEEF PIE

SERVES 6

INGREDIENTS

2 tablespoons vegetable oil

1 kg (2 lb) blade or topside steak, cubed

1 onion, chopped

2 tablespoons plain (all-purpose) flour

2 beef stock cubes, crumbled

1 teaspoon Vegemite or yeast extract

1 tablespoon tomato paste

½ teaspoon salt

¼ cup parsley, chopped

1 teaspoon Worcestershire sauce

Tabasco

250 g (8 oz) pre-made puff pastry

2 tablespoons milk

METHOD

. Heat oil in frying pan and brown the beef and onion, then transfer to slow cooker using a slotted spoon. Add the flour to the juices in the pan, brown it, and pour in 1 cup water. Add the stock cubes, Vegemite or yeast extract, tomato paste and salt and bring to the boil, stirring.

. Pour liquid into slow cooker with the parsley, Worcestershire sauce and Tabasco to taste, and cook on low for at least 6–8 hours or overnight. Test meat for tenderness, then spoon beef mixture into a greased pie dish and allow to cool.

. Preheat the oven to 190°C (375°F). Slice puff pastry into long strips. Brush rim of pie dish with a little milk and fit a pastry strip around the wet rim, then use remaining strips to create a lattice across the meat. Brush lightly with milk and bake pie for 25–30 minutes.

. Recipe makes one whole pie or 6 individual pies.

CHILLI BEEF TACOS

SERVES 6

INGREDIENTS

2 teaspoons vegetable oil

500 g (1 lb) minced beef

2 onions, chopped

60 g (2 oz) taco seasoning mix

½ teaspoon freshly ground black pepper

2 tablespoons tomato paste

125 ml (4 fl oz) beef stock

6 taco shells or corn tortillas

METHOD

. Heat the oil in a frying pan, and sauté the beef until browned. Add onion and cook until slightly softened. Stir in taco mix, pepper and tomato paste and cook for 1–2 minutes. Add stock and stir.

. Transfer mixture to slow cooker and cook for approximately 4 hours on low. If mixture is too wet at the end of the cooking time, remove the cooker lid and cook on high until liquid has reduced.

. Spoon beef mixture into heated taco shells or tortillas and serve at once with bowls of chopped tomatoes, cucumber and lettuce.

PORK

COUNTRY-STYLE PÂTÉ

SERVES 10

INGREDIENTS

500 g (1.1 lb) lean pork, minced

2 rashers bacon, finely diced

1 egg

2 tablespoons sour cream

¼ onion, minced

2 tablespoons brandy

1 tablespoon plain flour

2 cloves garlic, minced

grated zest of ½ lemon

½ teaspoon salt

½ teaspoon freshly ground black pepper

¼ teaspoon ground allspice

¼ teaspoon dried thyme

METHOD

. Mix together pork, bacon, egg, sour cream, onion, brandy, flour, garlic, lemon zest, salt, pepper, allspice and thyme.

. Oil a 500 g (1 lb) coffee can. Spoon meat mixture into the can and pat down. Cover with aluminium foil.

. Place a trivet in the bottom of the slow cooker and place can on trivet. Cover and cook on high for 2 hours, or until firm. Allow to cool, then chill in the refrigerator.

SLOW-BAKED PORK

SERVES 4

INGREDIENTS

1 kg (2.2 lb) boned shoulder of pork, rind removed

2 tablespoons olive oil

2 teaspoons dried thyme

2 teaspoons dried oregano

1 teaspoon dried rosemary

4 cloves garlic, sliced

zest of 1 lemon

250 ml (8 fl oz) chicken stock

salt and freshly ground black pepper

METHOD

. In a heavy-based frypan, brown the pork on all sides in the olive oil, then remove to the slow cooker. Place the herbs in the slow cooker, then add the lemon zest.

. Add the chicken stock and salt and pepper to taste. Cook on low for around 8–9 hours and the meat will come apart easily.

GLAZED HAM

SERVES 12

INGREDIENTS

2½ kg (5.5 lb) boneless ham

3 tablespoons orange marmalade

1 tablespoon Dijon mustard

METHOD

. Trim fat from ham. Mix together marmalade and mustard and spread on top of ham. Place in the slow cooker.

. Cover and cook on low for 6–8 hours. Transfer ham to a carving board. Pour meat juices into a sauce boat, skim off fat and serve sauce with the ham.

SPINACH AND PORK TERRINE

MAKES 1 LOAF

INGREDIENTS

300 g (10 oz) frozen chopped spinach

375 g (13 oz) lean minced pork

1 egg

2½ tablespoons brandy

¼ cup fresh parsley, chopped

¼ onion, finely minced

½ teaspoon salt

½ teaspoon dried thyme

½ teaspoon dried basil

¼ teaspoon ground nutmeg

¼ teaspoon freshly ground black pepper

¼ cup chopped olives

4 rashers bacon

60 g (2 oz) ham, sliced

1 bay leaf

METHOD

. Thaw spinach and squeeze dry. Place pork, egg, brandy, parsley and onion in a mixing bowl. Combine salt, thyme, basil, nutmeg and pepper. Add half of seasoning mixture to meat and mix well. Mix remaining seasoning mixture with spinach and olives.

. Line bottom and sides of a 10 x 18 cm (4 x 7 in) loaf pan (or pan that fits in your slow cooker) with bacon. Spread with one-third of the meat mixture. Cover with half the spinach and half the ham slices. Top with another third of the meat mixture and remaining spinach, ham and then finally with the remaining meat mixture. Place bay leaf on top.

. Cover with aluminium foil. Place a trivet in the bottom of the slow cooker and place loaf pan on trivet. Cook in the slow cooker on high for 2 hours. Chill, then slice to serve.

SWEDISH PORK MEATBALLS

SERVES 6

INGREDIENTS

1½ cups white breadcrumbs

250 ml (8 fl oz) buttermilk

500 g (1.1 lb) lean pork mince

250 g (8 oz) lean beef mince

2 eggs

1 medium onion, finely chopped

2 teaspoons salt

¾ teaspoon dill seeds

¼ teaspoon allspice

⅛ teaspoon ground nutmeg

60 g (2 oz) butter

250 ml (8 fl oz) chicken stock

125 ml (4 fl oz) dry white wine

freshly ground black pepper

250 ml (8 fl oz) cream

2 tablespoons fresh parsley leaves
   to garnish

METHOD

. Soak breadcrumbs in buttermilk for 5 minutes. Add meats, eggs, onion, salt, herbs and spices. Mix well, cover and refrigerate for 30 minutes.

. Shape tablespoon quantities of mixture into balls.

. Heat butter in a medium frypan and cook meatballs until lightly browned.

. Place meatballs into the slow cooker as they are browned. Add stock, wine and pepper. Cover and cook on low for 5 hours. Approximately 20 minutes before serving turn the heat to high and add cream.

. Serve meatballs garnished with parsley and accompanied by crusty bread.

Note: The meatballs will have a finer texture if the meats are minced together twice (ask your butcher to do this).

CONTINENTAL MEATBALLS

SERVES 6

INGREDIENTS

500 g (1.1 lb) minced pork

500 g (1.1 lb) minced veal

1 sachet onion soup

2 eggs

½ cup quick-cooking rolled oats

250 ml (8 fl oz) milk

¼ cup fresh parsley, chopped

salt and freshly ground black
   pepper

2 beef stock cubes, crumbled

¼ teaspoon ground nutmeg

¼ teaspoon ground allspice

125 ml (4 fl oz) beef stock

METHOD

. Preheat oven to 210°C (425°F). Place minced meats, onion soup, eggs, rolled oats, milk, parsley, salt, pepper, beef stock cubes, nutmeg and allspice in a mixing bowl. Mix until blended, then shape into 3 cm (1.2 in) balls.

. Place 25 mm (1 in) apart in a shallow baking dish. Bake for 15 minutes or until browned.

. Transfer to the slow cooker, pour in stock and cover. Cook on low for 1–2 hours.

. Serve with sour cream or yoghurt.

PULLED PORK ROLLERS

MAKES 20–24

INGREDIENTS

250 ml (8 fl oz) barbecue sauce

125 ml (4 fl oz) apple cider

125 ml (4 fl oz) beef stock

1 tablespoon Worcestershire sauce

1 large onion, diced

2 cloves garlic, crushed

1 teaspoon thyme

1 teaspoon chilli powder

2 kg (4.4 lb) pork shoulder

20–24 roller buns

Coleslaw, to serve

METHOD

. Combine all the ingredients except for the pork, buns and coleslaw in a bowl and stir. Pour half the sauce into a slow cooker, add the pork, then cover with the rest of the sauce.

. Cook, covered, on high heat for 5–6 hours or on low heat for 10 hours. Remove the meat from the slow cooker and pour the sauce into a small saucepan. Bring the sauce to the boil and reduce it until it thickens.

. Meanwhile, remove the bone from the pork and, using two forks, shred the meat. Put the meat and the thickened sauce back in the slow cooker to keep warm.

. Slice part-way through the buns lengthwise. To assemble the rollers, spoon in enough pork and sauce to fill it.

PORK AND PINEAPPLE CURRY

SERVES 6

INGREDIENTS

1 kg (2.2 lb) lean pork, cut into
   cubes
60 g (2 oz) plain flour
1 teaspoon salt
2 teaspoons olive oil
1 large onion, chopped
1 tablespoon curry powder
1 tablespoon paprika
1 L (2 pints) chicken stock
2 dried red chillies
1 tablespoon mango chutney
1 teaspoon Worcestershire sauce
500 g (18 oz) canned pineapple
   pieces
2 bay leaves

METHOD

. Toss the pork in the flour and salt.

. In a large heavy-based frypan, heat the oil and brown the meat.

. Lift out onto a plate with a draining spoon. In the same frypan, fry
the onions until soft. Stir in the curry powder and paprika. Fry for
2 minutes then return meat to the pan. Stir well and cook for a few
minutes.

. Add remaining ingredients, bring to the boil and transfer to slow
cooker. Cover and cook on high for
3–4 hours or on low for 6–8 hours. Remove bay leaves before
serving.

SPICY PORK WITH HERBS

SERVES 10

INGREDIENTS

1 tablespoon oil

1½ kg (3.3 lb) lean pork, cut into
   3 cm (1.2 in) cubes

2 medium onions, cut into wedges

2 green capsicums (bell peppers),
   cut into 25 mm pieces

1 clove garlic, minced

1 teaspoon seasoned salt

½ teaspoon dried oregano

½ teaspoon freshly ground black
   pepper

2 teaspoons cider vinegar

400 g (14 oz) canned tomatoes

2 tablespoons plain flour

METHOD

. Heat oil in a heavy-based frypan. Add pork and brown lightly on
  all sides.

. Transfer pork to slow cooker. Add onion, green capsicum, garlic,
  salt, oregano, pepper, vinegar and tomatoes, mix well.

. Cover and cook on low for 6–8 hours.

. Blend ¼ cup water and the flour until smooth

. Turn slow cooker to high and stir in flour mixture. Cook, stirring
  until thickened.

SWEET AND SOUR PORK

SERVES 6

INGREDIENTS

1 kg (2.2 lb) pork, cubed

1 onion, finely chopped

2 cloves garlic, crushed

1 red capsicum (bell pepper), sliced

1 green capsicum (bell pepper), sliced

1 stalk celery, chopped

1 bunch bok choy, chopped

400 g (14 oz) canned pineapple pieces in juice

MARINADE

2 tablespoons soy sauce

1 tablespoon brown sugar

1 tablespoon dry sherry

SAUCE

1 tablespoon cornflour

2 tablespoons soy sauce

2 tablespoons honey

1 tablespoon brown vinegar

1 pinch ground cinnamon

METHOD

. Place pork in a non-metallic bowl. Combine marinade ingredients and mix through pork. Refrigerate while you prepare the vegetables.

. Prepare the onion, garlic, red capsicum, green capsicum and celery and place in the slow cooker.

. Combine sauce ingredients. Add the sauce and the pork and marinade to the slow cooker, stir well and cook on low for 7–9 hours.

. After 4 hours, add the bok choy. With about 1 hour to go, add the pineapple and juice and stir through. Serve with rice or noodles.

PORK BELLY SLIDERS
WITH SPICY CHILLI SAUCE

MAKES 12

INGREDIENTS

1 kg (2.2 lb) boneless pork belly

250 ml (8 fl oz) water

60 g (2 oz) sugar

1–2 long red chillies, de-seeded

1 teaspoon fish sauce

1 tablespoon soy sauce

juice of half a lime

½ cup fresh coriander

salt and pepper to taste

12 brioche buns

METHOD

. Preheat the oven at 220°C (425°F).

. Score the pork belly skin at 1 cm (½ in) intervals. Place the pork on a rack in a roasting pan, skin-side up. Pat dry the pork belly with paper towel and rub salt into the skin. Pour water into the roasting pan, enough to fill the pan to just under the rack. Place in the oven and roast for 30 minutes or until the skin is crispy. Reduce the heat to 180°C (350°F) and roast for a further 1½ hours or until the meat is tender, topping up with water as necessary. Remove the pork and cut into squares to fit the buns.

. In a saucepan, bring the water and sugar to the boil. Boil until it starts to caramelise. Add the chillies, fish sauce and the soy sauce. Reduce the heat and simmer until the liquid has reduced by half. Squeeze in the lime juice then set aside for later use.

. Slice the buns in half lengthways.

. To assemble the sliders, add a piece of pork and drizzle over with some caramel dressing. Top with a few coriander leaves then the top bun. Hold together with a cocktail stick.

. Serve with your favorite side such as an Asian-style coleslaw.

ROAST PORK

SERVES 4–6

INGREDIENTS

3 kg (6.6 lb) loin leg of pork

salt, to taste

apple sauce, to serve

METHOD

. Preheat oven to 250°C (500°F). Rub pork with salt and place in a roasting pan.

. Cook pork in oven for 30 minutes to crisp crackling, then reduce heat to 160°C (325°F) and cook for three hours.

. Continue to baste from time to time throughout the cooking time.

. When pork is cooked, place on a carving tray and keep warm. Make gravy from pan juices.

. Serve roast pork with apple sauce, roast potatoes and roast vegetables.

SEAFOOD

CURRIED SCALLOPS

SERVES 6

INGREDIENTS

250 g (8 oz) scallops

125 ml (4 fl oz) dry white wine

1 bouquet garni

125 g (4 oz) butter

310 ml (10 fl oz) cups thin cream

½ teaspoon curry powder

salt and freshly ground black
pepper

2 egg yolks

2 tablespoons milk

METHOD

.   Place scallops, white wine and bouquet garni in the slow cooker and cook on low for approximately 1 hour. Pour off and reserve liquid, discard bouquet garni and keep scallops warm in slow cooker.

.   Put cooking liquid with butter into a small saucepan and boil hard to reduce. Stir in the cream, curry powder and salt and pepper, and again boil hard for 2–3 minutes. Remove from heat and allow to cool.

.   Beat egg yolks with milk, and carefully stir into cooled cream mixture. Pour mixture back into slow cooker with the scallops and cook on high for 45–60 minutes. To serve, place a little cooked rice in a small bowl and spoon over 3–4 scallops with a generous quantity of sauce. Serve immediately.

CIOPPINO

SERVES 8

INGREDIENTS

500 g (18 oz) sea bass, cubed

250 g (8 oz) mushrooms, sliced

2 carrots, sliced

1 onion, chopped

1 green capsicum (bell pepper), chopped

1 large clove garlic, minced

500 g (18 oz) tomato pasta sauce

500 ml (1 pint) fish stock

1 teaspoon salt

½ teaspoon freshly ground black pepper

½ teaspoon dried oregano

250 g (8 oz) cooked clams

250 g (8 oz) cooked prawns (shrimp)

500 g (16 oz) cooked crab meat

¼ cup parsley, chopped

METHOD

. Combine sea bass, mushrooms, vegetables, garlic, tomato sauce, fish stock and seasonings in slow cooker.

. Cover and cook on low for 10–12 hours. Approximately 30 minutes before finished cooking, turn to high and stir in remaining seafood. Garnish with parsley before serving.

Note: This rustic tomato and fish stew is referred to as 'cioppino' in Italy. Serve with fresh crusty bread and a good red wine.

TROUT IN WINE SAUCE

SERVES 4

INGREDIENTS

4 trout, cleaned
125 g (4 oz) mushrooms, sliced
125 ml (4 fl oz) white wine
grated zest and juice of 1 lemon
freshly ground black pepper
¼ tablespoon salt
125 ml (4 fl oz) crème fraîche

METHOD

. Grease the slow cooker with a little olive oil and place the trout tail to head in the bottom of the slow cooker.

. Add the sliced mushrooms, wine, lemon zest and juice, black pepper and salt. Cover and cook on low for about 3–4 hours.

. Stir in the crème fraîche and heat a further 15 minutes.

FISH AND TOMATOES

SERVES 4

INGREDIENTS

2 fish fillets (bream or cod)

plain flour

**salt and freshly ground black
 pepper**

4 tablespoons vegetable oil

**2 onions, peeled and finely
 chopped**

**400 g (14 oz) canned chopped
 tomatoes**

1 tablespoon tomato purée

125 ml (4 fl oz) fish stock

cayenne pepper

METHOD

. Cut the fish into sections to fit into the slow cooker.

. Season the flour with salt and pepper and coat each piece of fish.

. Heat the oil in a heavy-based frypan and quickly fry each piece of
  fish, then put the fish into the slow cooker.

. Fry the onions until softened and mix in the tomatoes, tomato
  purée and stock. Bring the sauce to the boil and taste, then season
  with cayenne.

. Pour the sauce over the fish and cook on low for 4–6 hours.

BOUILLABAISSE

SERVES 6

INGREDIENTS

3 kg (6.6 lb) mixed fish and
 seafood, including firm white
 fish fillets, prawns (shrimp),
 mussels, crab and calamari rings

60 ml (2 fl oz) olive oil

2 cloves garlic, crushed

2 large onions, chopped

2 leeks, sliced

2 x 400 g (14 oz) canned tomatoes

150 ml (5 fl oz) fish stock

1 tablespoon chopped fresh thyme
 or 1 teaspoon dried thyme

2 tablespoons chopped fresh basil
 or 1½ teaspoons dried basil

2 tablespoons chopped fresh
 parsley

2 bay leaves

2 tablespoons finely grated orange
 rind

1 teaspoon saffron threads

150 ml (5 fl oz) dry white wine

freshly ground black pepper

METHOD

. Remove the bones and skin from the fish fillets and cut into 2 cm
(¾ in) cubes. Peel and devein the prawns, leaving the tails intact.
Scrub and remove the beards from the mussels. Cut the crab into
quarters. Set aside.

. Heat a slow cooker on a high setting, then add the oil, garlic,
onions, leeks, tomatoes and stock and cook for 1½ hours. Add the
thyme, basil, parsley, bay leaves, orange rind, saffron and wine.
Cook for 30 minutes.

. Add the fish and crab and cook for 1 hour. Add the remaining
seafood and cook for 1 hour longer or until all fish and seafood are
cooked. Season to taste with black pepper.

THAI SEAFOOD CURRY

SERVES 8

INGREDIENTS

1 tablespoon red curry paste

400 ml (13 fl oz) unsweetened
  coconut milk

5 cm (2 in) piece ginger, grated

juice of 2 large limes

1 large carrot, grated

100 g (3½ in) purple cabbage,
  shredded

1 red onion, coarsely chopped

5 cloves garlic, coarsely chopped

2 tablespoons oyster sauce

1 bunch Thai basil, chopped

60 g (2 oz) butter

4 tablespoons olive oil

750 g (1 lb 8 oz) clams, rinsed in
  salted water several times until
  water runs clear

500 g (18 oz) king prawns
  (shrimp), cleaned and deveined

500 g (18 oz) scallops

METHOD

. Preheat slow cooker for 20 minutes on high.

. Place curry paste in bottom of slow cooker, add coconut milk and stir with whisk to combine.

. Blend in ginger, half the lime juice and ½ cup water. Add carrot, cabbage, onion and garlic.

. Cook for 3 hours on high or 6 hours on low. During the last half hour of cooking, add remaining lime juice, oyster sauce, salt, and basil.

. Heat half the butter and half the olive oil in a heavy-based frypan fitted with a lid. Cook clams until they open, discarding any that do not and place in slow cooker.

. Sauté prawns and scallops in remaining butter and oil on medium-high heat until just cooked, turning just as prawns turn pink and scallops turn golden brown. Add to slow cooker.

. Heat through and season to taste. Serve over rice and peas. Garnish with more freshly torn Thai basil.

INDIVIDUAL CLAM BAKES

SERVES 4

INGREDIENTS

500 g (18 oz) clam meat

4 eggs, beaten

40 g (1½ oz) butter, melted

90 ml (3 fl oz) milk

1 teaspoon salt

½ onion, diced

⅓ green capsicum (bell pepper), diced

60 g (2 oz) breadcrumbs

METHOD

. Combine all ingredients. Spoon into 4 individual dishes and place in the slow cooker. Cover and cook on low for 5–6 hours.

KEDGEREE

SERVES 4

INGREDIENTS

500 g (18 oz) smoked trout or cod
30 g (1 oz) butter
1 onion, finely sliced
1 teaspoon curry powder
1 cup basmati rice
1 leek, diced, washed
500 ml (1 pint) boiling water
1 sachet Japanese dashi stock
30 ml (1 fl oz) cream
2 hard-boiled eggs, coarsely
   chopped
freshly ground black pepper
2 tablespoons chopped fresh
   parsley

METHOD

. Place smoked fish in a saucepan, cover with cold water and bring slowly to the simmer. Cook for 6 minutes, drain and flake.

. Melt butter in a large frypan over a medium heat and fry onion until soft. Add curry powder and cook, stirring, for 2 minutes. Add rice and leeks and fry gently for 5 minutes, stirring, until rice is translucent yet slightly brown in color.

. Place rice mixture in a slow cooker and add boiling water, dashi stock and flaked fish. Gently stir to combine all ingredients, cover and cook on high for 2 hours.

. When ready to serve add cream and eggs and toss gently with a fork. Season to taste with freshly ground black pepper. Sprinkle with parsley. Serve with lemon wedges if desired.

SLOW-COOKED JAMBALAYA

SERVES 8

INGREDIENTS

500 g (18 oz) boneless chicken breasts, cut into 25 mm (1 in) cubes

300 g (10½ oz) smoked sausage, sliced

½ onion, chopped

1 green capsicum (bell pepper), chopped

800 g (1 lb 10 oz) canned crushed tomatoes

250 ml (8 fl oz) chicken stock

125 ml (4 fl oz) dry white wine

2 teaspoons dried oregano

2 teaspoons dried parsley flakes

2 teaspoons Cajun seasoning

1 teaspoon cayenne pepper

500 g (18 oz) cooked prawns (shrimp)

2 cups white rice, cooked

METHOD

. Combine chicken, sausage, onion, and capsicum in slow cooker.

. Add tomatoes, chicken stock, wine, oregano, parsley, Cajun seasoning and pepper and stir gently.

. Cover and cook on low for 6–8 hours or on high for 3–4 hours. About 30–45 minutes before eating, add cooked prawns and hot cooked rice. Heat thoroughly before serving.

SEAFOOD AND TOMATO HERB RAGÙ

SERVES 6

INGREDIENTS

800 g (1 lb 10 oz) canned crushed
   tomatoes

1 teaspoon salt

250 g (8 oz) tomato pasta sauce

1 leek, chopped

½ stalk celery, chopped

250 ml (8 fl oz) white wine

60 ml (2 fl oz) extra virgin olive
   oil

3 cloves garlic, minced

125 g (4 oz) fresh parsley,
   chopped

1 small green capsicum (bell
   pepper), deseeded and chopped

4 sprigs fresh thyme, leaves
   removed and stalks discarded

60 g (2 oz) fresh basil, chopped

4 sprigs fresh oregano, leaves
   removed and chopped

½ teaspoon ground paprika

¼ teaspoon crushed red chilli

500 g (18 oz) firm white fish
   fillets, cubed

12 prawns (shrimp), shelled and
   deveined and shelled

12 scallops

METHOD

. Combine 1 cup water with all of the ingredients except the seafood
  in the slow cooker. Stir to blend.

. Cover and cook on high for 3–4 hours or on low for 6–8 hours.

. About 15–30 minutes before serving, add the seafood and cook
  until seafood is just cooked through. Garnish with parsley to serve.

SHELLFISH AND CHORIZO PAELLA

SERVES 6

INGREDIENTS

30 ml (1 fl oz) extra virgin olive
  oil

500 g (18 oz) chorizo sausages,
  casings removed

1 green capsicum (bell pepper),
  chopped

1 medium red onion, chopped

4 cloves garlic, minced

½ teaspoon crushed red pepper
  flakes

2½ cups long-grain white rice

500 ml (1 pint) clam juice or fish
  stock

250 ml (8 fl oz) tomato juice

250 ml (8 fl oz) dry white wine

¼ teaspoon ground turmeric

¼ teaspoon freshly ground black
  pepper

1 teaspoon salt

½ teaspoon dried basil

375 g (13 oz) canned artichoke
  hearts, drained

12 small hard-shell clams in the
  shell, rinsed and scrubbed

500 g (18 oz) medium raw prawns
  (shrimp), shelled and deveined

500 g (18 oz) cooked crab legs, in
  the shell, cracked

METHOD

. Heat oil in a heavy-based frypan on medium heat, add sausage meat and cook the until no pink remains, about 10 minutes. Break up the meat with a wooden spoon as it cooks. Drain any fat that accumulates.

. Combine the cooked meat and ½ cup water with all other ingredients except the seafood in the slow cooker and cook covered on high for 4–6 hours, stirring twice.

. Thirty minutes before serving, add the clams and prawns on top of the paella. Arrange the crab legs on top of the other shellfish and cover again.

. Cook on high until the clams open, about 20–30 minutes. Discard any unopened clams.

. To serve, ladle equal portions of the paella into large bowls and serve while hot.

SALMON POACHED IN WINE

SERVES 4

INGREDIENTS

1 kg (2.2 lb) salmon fillet
250 (8 fl oz) white wine
1 bay leaf
1 sprig parsley
¼ teaspoon salt
freshly ground black pepper
juice and grated zest of 1 lemon

METHOD

. Brush the inside of the slow cooker with olive oil.

. Rinse the salmon fillet and dry with absorbent paper. Place the fillet in the bottom of the slow cooker.

. Add the wine, bay leaf, parsley, salt, pepper, lemon juice and zest. Cover and cook on low for 3–4 hours.

. Serve either hot or cold. This dish is delicious cold with a salad and crispy bread and butter.

CORN AND TUNA BAKE

SERVES 6–8

INGREDIENTS

400 g (14 oz) canned corn kernels, drained

¼ red capsicum (bell pepper), chopped

400 g (14 oz) canned tuna, drained

120 g (4 oz) mushrooms, chopped

250 ml (8 fl oz) thin cream

250 g (8 oz) Cheddar cheese, grated

¼ cup parsley, chopped

250 g (8 oz) wholemeal macaroni

TOPPING

1 cup soft wholemeal breadcrumbs

45 g (1½ oz) butter, melted

30 g (1 oz) Parmesan cheese, grated

1 teaspoon dried basil

METHOD

. Bring a large saucepan of salted water to the boil, add the macaroni and cook for 8 minutes or until just firm in the centre (al dente). Drain, set aside and keep warm.

. Place soup, corn, red capsicum, tuna, mushrooms, cream, cheese and parsley in slow cooker. Mix together and cook on high for 1 hour or on low for about 2 hours, until vegetables have softened.

. Preheat the oven to 190°C (375°F). Pour tuna mixture into a greased casserole together with macaroni. Mix thoroughly.

. To make the breadcrumb topping, mix all ingredients together. Sprinkle topping over casserole and bake for 30 minutes or until top is golden brown.

VEGETABLES

KIDNEY BEANS IN PLUM SAUCE

SERVES 4

INGREDIENTS

200 g (7 oz) dried red kidney beans

620 ml (20 fl oz) water

1 tablespoon chopped fresh basil

1 tablespoon chopped fresh coriander (cilantro), plus extra leaves to garnish

1 tablespoon chopped fresh parsley

¼ teaspoon cayenne pepper

salt to taste

1 small clove garlic

⅓ cup plum jam

2 teaspoons red wine vinegar

METHOD

. Rinse kidney beans well in a strainer under running water. Add the beans and water to a slow cooker set on high. Cook for 2½ hours.

. Meanwhile, place the basil, coriander, parsley, cayenne pepper, salt and garlic in a food processor and blend to a paste. Add the jam and vinegar and pulse to combine.

. After 2½ hours add the paste to the beans and stir gently to coat the beans with the dressing. Turn slow cooker onto low and cook for 1 more hour to allow flavors to penetrate. Garnish with coriander leaves. Can be served warm or at room temperature.

SAVORY ZUCCHINI CUSTARDS

SERVES 4

INGREDIENTS

30 g (1 oz) butter

¼ cup white onion, finely chopped

250 g (8 oz) zucchini (courgette), grated

salt and freshly ground black pepper

60 g (2 oz) Parmesan cheese, grated

60 g (2 oz) Cheddar cheese, grated

90 ml (3 fl oz) thickened cream

2 large eggs, beaten

METHOD

. Heat butter in a frying pan and sauté onions for 10–15 minutes until tender and just beginning to brown.

. Tip zucchini into clean absorbent paper and squeeze dry. Increase the heat in the pan, add the zucchini and toss for 5 minutes or so. Cover pan and cook for several minutes longer over low heat, until zucchini is tender. Season to taste and pour into a bowl.

. Add cheese to the bowl, pour in cream and stir well. Fold eggs into mixture, then taste and adjust seasoning if necessary. (The mixture may be refrigerated at this stage until ready to cook. If you do this, allow a longer cooking time.)

. Grease 4 small ramekins and pour custard into each. Put dishes into slow cooker, and pour enough water into the base of the cooker to come approximately halfway up the sides of the dishes. Cook on low for 1 hour with lid ajar.

. Cook, covered, for another 3 hours, testing for firmness at the end of that time.

. Test for firmness by inserting a knife blade into one of the custards – the blade should come out clean.

SPINACH CUSTARDS

SERVES 6–8

INGREDIENTS

250 g (8 oz) cooked spinach or
  silverbeet, stems removed
120 g (4 oz) cream cheese
2 small eggs
100 ml (3½ fl oz) milk
1 small onion, peeled and
  chopped
¼ teaspoon salt
freshly ground black pepper
½ teaspoon dried basil
30 g (1 oz) Parmesan cheese,
  grated
8 fresh basil sprigs

METHOD

. Drain spinach or silverbeet until as dry as possible, then process in a food processor or blender until finely chopped. Add remaining ingredients and half the basil and blend until very smooth.

. Pour mixture into 6–8 small, buttered ovenproof dishes and cover each with aluminium foil. Place dishes in the slow cooker and pour a little water into base, then cook on high for approximately 1½ hours or on low for 2½ hours.

. To serve, sprinkle with extra grated cheese and garnish with a basil sprig.

. This dish makes a delicious light lunch served with a salad and fresh, warm bread.

VEGETABLE CASSEROLE

SERVES 8

INGREDIENTS

500 g (1 lb) potatoes, peeled and thickly sliced

500 g (1 lb) very ripe tomatoes, peeled and sliced

½ teaspoon sugar

2 white onions, thinly sliced

2 green or red capsicums (bell peppers), thinly sliced

1 kg (2.2 lb) small zucchini (courgette), sliced

salt and freshly ground black pepper

1 clove garlic, crushed

1 teaspoon dried basil

30 g (1 oz) butter

30 g (1 oz) Parmesan cheese, grated

¼ cup parsley, chopped

METHOD

. Boil the potatoes until slightly tender. Sprinkle the tomatoes with sugar.

. Grease the base of the slow cooker and layer in the vegetables, starting with the onion. Sprinkle each layer with salt, pepper, garlic and basil. Finish with a layer of tomatoes, then dot with butter. Pour over any juice from tomato slices.

. Cook on high for approximately 3 hours or on low for approximately 5 hours. Serve sprinkled with grated cheese and parsley.

VEGETABLE CURRY

SERVES 4–6

INGREDIENTS

30 ml (1 fl oz) vegetable oil

1 kg (2.2 lb) leeks, thinly sliced
and washed

500 g (1 lb) baby carrots,
scrubbed and sliced diagonally

4 stalks celery, finely chopped

½ clove garlic, crushed

1 tablespoon curry powder

180 ml (6 fl oz) vegetable stock

2 teaspoons cornflour
(cornstarch)

salt and freshly ground black
pepper

6 spring onions (scallions), sliced
diagonally

METHOD

. Heat the oil in a frying pan and lightly sauté the leeks, carrots
and celery. Spoon vegetables into slow cooker. Add garlic and
curry powder to frying pan and cook for 1–2 minutes.

. Blend stock with cornflour (cornstarch), add to frying pan and
bring to the boil, stirring constantly. Pour mixture into slow
cooker and season. Cook on low for approximately 4 hours or
on high for approximately 2–3 hours (test for tenderness after
this, as cooking time can very greatly according to the tenderness
of the vegetables).

. When vegetables are cooked, add spring onions. Serve with rice.

LEEKS WITH BEANS

SERVES 6

INGREDIENTS

250 g (8 oz) dried black eyed
  (navy) beans, soaked overnight

15 ml (½ fl oz) vegetable oil

1 large onion, chopped

2 cloves garlic, crushed

500 g (1 lb) leeks, sliced and
  washed

¼ cup parsley, chopped

6 tomatoes, peeled, deseeded and
  chopped

1 tablespoon raw sugar

1 teaspoon mustard powder

2 bay leaves

½ teaspoon dried marjoram

1 tablespoon tomato paste

60 ml (2 fl oz) vegetable stock

salt and freshly ground black
  pepper

METHOD

. Drain the beans well. Heat the oil in a frying pan and sauté the
  onion and garlic, then add the leeks and sauté until softened.
  Spoon leek mixture, beans and all remaining ingredients into slow
  cooker.

. Cover and cook on low for approximately 8–9 hours or on high for
  4–5 hours. Garnish with extra parsley.

HERBED CANNELLONI WITH TOMATO SAUCE

SERVES 3–4

INGREDIENTS

250 g (8 oz) cottage cheese

30 g (1 oz) Parmesan cheese, grated

1 teaspoon mixed dried herbs

6 spring onions (scallions), finely chopped

salt and freshly ground black pepper

few drops Angostura bitters (optional)

8 instant cannelloni tubes

TOMATO SAUCE

250 ml (8 fl oz) tomato purée

3–4 spring onions (scallions), chopped

2 teaspoons Worcestershire sauce

4 drops Angostura bitters

1 large clove garlic, crushed

METHOD

. Bring a large saucepan of salted water to the boil, add the pasta tubes and cook for 8 minutes or until just firm in the centre (al dente). Drain, set aside and keep warm. Place the cheeses, herbs, spring onions, salt and pepper and bitters in a bowl and mix thoroughly.

. To make the sauce, mix together all ingredients.

. Lightly butter the base of the slow cooker. Spoon cheese mixture into cannelloni tubes. Spoon a little tomato sauce into the cooker, then arrange the stuffed cannelloni tubes in the cooker and spoon over remainder of sauce. Cook for 1–1½ hours on high or 2–2½ hours on low. Serve sprinkled with extra Parmesan cheese and parsley sprigs.

STUFFED VINE LEAVES IN TOMATO SAUCE

SERVES 4

INGREDIENTS

12 grape vine leaves, canned or
  fresh

2 cups cooked brown rice

1 teaspoon dried mixed herbs

pinch of nutmeg

salt and freshly ground black
  pepper

1 teaspoon dried garlic

2 tomatoes, chopped and peeled

¼ cup parsley, chopped

½ teaspoon Angostura bitters
  (optional)

2 spring onions (scallions),
  chopped finely

TOMATO SAUCE

15 g (½ oz) butter

1 onion, diced

400 g (14 oz) canned Roma
  tomatoes, drained and chopped

2 teaspoons brown sugar

pinch of dried herbs

15 g (½ oz) tomato paste

50 ml (1½ fl oz) dry red wine

¼ cup parsley, chopped

METHOD

. If you are using fresh vine leaves, remove the stems, pour boiling
water over leaves and leave for 1–2 minutes until softened. Dry,
and lightly wipe over each leaf with a drop of oil.

. Combine all other ingredients to make the filling. Squeeze a
handful of filling to make it firm and place onto leaf, then fold
into neat little parcel, sealing with a little squeeze. Repeat with
remaining leaves. Arrange carefully in base of slow cooker.

. To make the tomato sauce, heat the butter in a frying pan and
cook the onion until golden brown. Add all other ingredients and
cook until blended. Spoon sauce into slow cooker over vine leaf
parcels, and cook on high for approximately 1½ hours or on low
for 2–2½ hours.

PIZZA WITH SLOW-COOKED TOMATO SAUCE

SERVES 6–8

SAUCE

750 g (1½ lb) soft ripe tomatoes, peeled and chopped

30 ml (1 fl oz) tomato paste

few dashes Angostura bitters

1 small white onion, finely chopped

salt and freshly ground black pepper

1 teaspoon sugar

¼ teaspoon dried garlic

½ teaspoon mixed herbs

PIZZA DOUGH

1 tablespoon compressed yeast

1 teaspoon white sugar

500 g (1 lb) plain (all-purpose) flour

pinch of salt

15 g (½ oz) butter

15 ml (½ fl oz) vegetable oil

METHOD

. Combine all sauce ingredients in slow cooker and allow to cook on low overnight. If the mixture is too thin the next morning, turn cooker to high and cook, uncovered, until thickened and reduced. Allow to cool.

. To make the dough, crumble the yeast into a bowl, stir in sugar and 1¼ cups lukewarm water until yeast has dissolved, sprinkle a little of the flour onto surface and set aside in a warm place until mixture froths.

. Sift the flour and salt together and rub in butter. Pour in frothy yeast mixture and mix with a wooden spoon, then turn out onto a floured board and knead for at least 5 minutes. Shape into a round and set aside in a warm place until dough has doubled in size.

. Preheat the oven to 220°C (425°F). Roll dough out thinly, place on greased pizza tray or heated pizza stone and prick surface all over with a fork.

. Brush pizza with vegetable oil and spread generously with tomato sauce. Add preferred pizza toppings (for example, cheeses, olives, basil), then place pizza in oven and cook for about 50 minutes.

ARGENTINEAN BEAN AND VEGETABLE STEW

SERVES 4

INGREDIENTS

15 ml (½ fl oz) olive oil

1 onion, finely diced

2 cloves garlic, crushed

1 red capsicum (bell pepper), diced

1 jalapeño chilli, deseeded and diced

1 teaspoon sweet paprika

400 g (14 oz) canned diced tomatoes

500 ml (1 pint) vegetable stock

250 g (8 oz) new potatoes, quartered

250 g (8 oz) sweet potato, diced

1 carrot, sliced

400 g (14 oz) canned cannellini beans, rinsed and drained

200 g (7 oz) Savoy cabbage, shredded

¼ cup fresh coriander (cilantro), chopped

salt and freshly ground black pepper

METHOD

. Heat oil in a large frying pan over medium heat. Cook onion, garlic, capsicum and chilli until soft. Add sweet paprika and cook until aromatic.

. Transfer contents of frying pan to a slow cooker set on high and add tomatoes and vegetable stock. Stir to combine, then add potato, sweet potato and carrot. Bring to the boil. Reduce heat to low, cover, and simmer for 1½ hours until vegetables are tender.

. Add beans, cabbage and coriander (cilantro) and season with salt and pepper. Simmer for a further 30 minutes or until cabbage is cooked.

. This dish is delicious with crusty bread.

EGGPLANT AND TOMATO CASSEROLE

SERVES 4

INGREDIENTS

1 medium eggplant (aubergine),
  cubed

250 g (8 oz) tomatoes, sliced

2 cloves garlic, crushed

¼ teaspoon Cayenne pepper or
  dash of Tabasco

1 cm (½ in) ginger, grated

1 teaspoon ground coriander

2 bay leaves

1 tablespoon raw sugar

125 ml (4 fl oz) natural yoghurt

METHOD

. Cover eggplant with a handful of salt and allow to stand for
  approximately an hour. Rinse and drain well.

. Combine eggplant with all remaining ingredients except yoghurt.
  Spoon into slow cooker and cook on low for approximately 4
  hours. Test to see whether eggplant is cooked.

. Turn setting to high, stir in the yoghurt and heat through.
  Remove bay leaves and serve. Each serving may be sprinkled with
  wholemeal breadcrumbs fried in a little butter, if desired.

DESSERTS

APRICOT MOUSSE

SERVES 4

INGREDIENTS

250 g (8 oz) dried apricots

2 floury cooking apples, peeled and thinly sliced

juice and zest of 1 lemon

¼ cup raw sugar

3 egg whites

125 ml (4 fl oz) thickened cream, whipped

METHOD

. Soak dried apricots for approximately 1 hour, then drain well. Place into slow cooker with apples, lemon juice and zest and sugar. Cook on low for 3–4 hours or on high for 2–3 hours, until apricots are soft and apples cooked. Drain fruit, discarding liquid, and purée in a blender or food processor. Chill.

. Beat egg whites until stiff. Beat the cream in a separate bowl, then fold half the cream into the egg whites. Carefully fold egg white mixture and remaining cream through the fruit purée. Chill.

BUTTERSCOTCH AND APRICOT PARFAIT

SERVES 4–6

INGREDIENTS

500 g (1 lb) fresh apricots

1 tablespoon sugar

1 cinnamon stick

pinch of ground nutmeg

**1–2 ripe mangoes, peeled and
   sliced**

**125 ml (4 fl oz) thickened cream,
   whipped**

4 sprigs mint

BUTTERSCOTCH CUSTARD

4 egg yolks

**400 g (14 oz) canned evaporated
   skim milk**

1 teaspoon vanilla extract

1 heaped tablespoon dark sugar

METHOD

. To make the custard, beat together all the ingredients until sugar
  has dissolved, then pour into a greased heatproof basin. Cover
  basin tightly with foil, place in slow cooker, and pour enough
  water into cooker to come halfway up the sides of the basin. Cook
  on low for 3–4 hours.

. Remove basin from slow cooker, loosen around the rim of the
  basin with a knife and slip custard onto a warmed plate.

. Wash and stone the apricots, then place them in the slow cooker
  with sugar, cinnamon stick, nutmeg, and
  1 tablespoon water to prevent sticking. Cook on high for at least 2
  hours, until tender and almost mushy. Remove cinnamon stick and
  drain fruit.

. Set aside 4–6 mango slices for garnish, then layer apricots,
  butterscotch custard and mangoes in tall parfait glasses until full.
  Top each glass with a swirl of cream.

HOT CARAMEL MERINGUE DESSERT

SERVES 4–6

INGREDIENTS

¼ cup raw sugar

375 ml (12 fl oz) evaporated milk

1 teaspoon vanilla extract

3 thick slices wholemeal bread,
  crusts removed, cubed

⅓ cup sultanas (golden raisins)

⅓ cup raisins, chopped

zest of 1 orange, grated

3 eggs, separated

60 ml (2 fl oz) thin cream

1 teaspoon lemon juice

⅓ cup caster sugar

1 teaspoon dried coconut

METHOD

. Place sugar in a heavy-based saucepan and heat over low temperature, stirring gently until sugar has dissolved. Once melted, increase heat and allow to cook without stirring until a deep golden brown. Remove from heat.

. Meanwhile, bring the milk to the boil. Pour boiling milk into the toffee gradually, stirring or whisking constantly to form a smooth caramel. Add vanilla.

. Mix together bread cubes, dried fruits and orange zest. Add caramel and allow to stand for about half an hour.

. Beat egg yolks and cream, and add lemon juice. Stir gently into cooling caramel mixture. Allow to become cold, then pour into an ovenproof basin, cover with foil and tie firmly with kitchen string. Fill the slow cooker with about 5 cm (2 in) of water and put in the basin. Cook on low for 2½–3 hours. Remove pudding basin, take off foil covering and allow to cool.

. Preheat the oven to 200°C (400°F). Whip the egg whites, gradually adding the sugar, then swirl meringue onto top of cooled pudding and sprinkle with coconut. Place in oven and cook for 15–20 minutes or until meringue is golden brown and crisp.

APPLE-NUT CHEESECAKE

SERVES 6–8

CRUST

1 cup cracker crumbs

½ teaspoon ground cinnamon

2 tablespoons sugar

40 g (1½ oz) butter, melted

¼ cup finely chopped pecans or walnuts

FILLING

500 ml (1 pint) cream cheese

¼ cup brown sugar

½ cup white sugar

2 large eggs

50 ml (1½ fl oz) double cream

1 tablespoon cornflour

1 teaspoon vanilla extract

TOPPING

1 large apple, thinly sliced

1 teaspoon cinnamon

¼ cup sugar

METHOD

. Combine crust ingredients and pat into an 18 cm (7 in) springform cake tin.

. To make the filling, beat sugars into cream cheese until smooth and creamy. Beat in eggs, cream, cornflour, and vanilla. Beat for about 3 minutes on medium speed with a hand-held electric mixer. Pour mixture onto the prepared crust.

. To make the topping, combine apple slices with sugar, cinnamon and nuts and place evenly over the top of cheesecake.

. Place the cheesecake on a rack in the slow cooker.

. Cover and cook on high for 2½–3 hours. Turn off the heat and let stand in the covered pot for about 1–2 hours until cool enough to handle.

. Cool thoroughly before removing pan sides. Chill before serving.

COUNTRY CURRANT PIE

SERVES 6–8

INGREDIENTS

340 g (12 oz) currants
½ cup sugar
1 tablespoon cornflour
juice and zest of 1 lemon

PASTRY
150 g (5 oz) butter
1½ cups plain flour
1½ teaspoons baking powder

METHOD

. To make the pastry, place the butter in a large bowl, pour in 30 ml (1 fl oz) boiling water and mash the butter slightly. Sift in the flour and baking powder and stir until mixture comes together, adding a little more flour if necessary until pastry is smooth and manageable. Allow to stand until firm and easy to handle.

. Combine currants, sugar, cornflour and lemon juice and zest with 125 ml (4 fl oz) water in the slow cooker. Cook for around 1 hour on high (this filling must be cooked on high to ensure the cornflour cells burst and thicken it). Allow to cool.

. Preheat the oven to 200°C (400°F). Reserve one-third of the pastry for the pie crust and roll out the remainder roughly on a floured board. Grease a 20 cm (8 in) pie dish and press pastry into the base and sides, then spoon in the currant filling.

. Roll the reserved pastry out between two sheets of baking paper. Peel off one sheet of the paper, invert the pastry onto the pie, then remove the remaining sheet. Pinch the pie edges together, trim any excess, and use the pastry scraps to create a decoration for the crust.

. Sprinkle with caster sugar and bake for approximately 45–50 minutes. Serve with cream.

CREAMY RICE PUDDING

SERVES 6

INGREDIENTS

zest of 1 orange, grated

2½ cups cooked rice

250 ml (8 fl oz) evaporated milk
or 250 ml (8 fl oz) ordinary
milk plus 1 beaten egg

⅔ cup raw sugar

60 g (2 oz) butter, softened

½ teaspoon vanilla extract

½ teaspoon ground cinnamon or
nutmeg

⅓ cup sultanas (golden raisins)

METHOD

. Reserve a little orange zest to garnish, then mix the rice with all other ingredients. Lightly grease the slow cooker interior and spoon in pudding mixture.

. Cook on high for approximately 1–2 hours or on low for 4–6 hours. Stir occasionally during first hour of cooking. Serve with a little cream and a pinch of grated orange zest.

GRAND MARNIER CRÈME CARAMEL

SERVES 4

INGREDIENTS

6 tablespoons white sugar
3 eggs
625 ml (1 pint 4 fl oz) milk
30 ml (1 fl oz) Grand Marnier

METHOD

. Melt half the sugar slowly in a heavy saucepan. Do not stir, just allow to melt into toffee.

. Butter 4 small heatproof crème caramel moulds, then pour the melted sugar quickly into base of dishes and swirl around the sides as high as possible.

. Beat eggs well and whisk into milk with Grand Marnier and the remaining sugar. Keep whisking until sugar has dissolved, then pour mixture into caramel moulds and cover with foil. Place moulds into slow cooker and pour sufficient cold water around the bases to come halfway up the sides. Cook on low for approximately 3–4 hours.

. Remove crème caramels from slow cooker and chill thoroughly. Serve either in the moulds or very carefully turned out onto plates, with any caramel left behind spooned over the top.

PRALINE CHEESECAKE

SERVES 6–8

CRUST

1 cup digestive biscuits, crumbled
¼ cup finely chopped pecans
2 tablespoons brown sugar
40 g (1½ oz) butter, melted

FILLING

500 ml (1 pint) cream cheese, at room temperature
¾ cup brown sugar
2 large eggs
60 ml (2 fl oz) thickened cream
1 teaspoon vanilla extract
1 tablespoon plain flour

METHOD

. To make the crust, combine crumbs and nuts with brown sugar and mix in melted butter until well moistened. Pat into an 18 cm (7 in) springform cake tin.

. To make the filling, beat cream cheese and sugar together until smooth. Add the eggs, cream, vanilla and flour. Beat for 3–4 minutes at medium speed with a hand-held electric mixer. Pour onto the prepared crust and place on a rack in the slow cooker. Cover and cook on high for 2½–3 hours. Turn off and leave for 1–2 hours until cool enough to remove.

. Cool completely and remove the sides of the pan. Garnish with pecan halves if desired. Chill before serving, and store leftovers in the refrigerator.

APPLE AND RAISIN SHORTIES

MAKES 10–12

INGREDIENTS

**500 g (1 lb) cooking apples,
    peeled and thinly sliced**

¼ cup raw sugar

4 cloves

½ cup raisins

zest of 1 lemon

squeeze of lemon juice

PASTRY

150 g (5 oz) butter

**250 g (8 oz) plain (all-purpose)
    flour**

8 teaspoons wholemeal flour

½ teaspoon baking powder

½ teaspoon cinnamon

METHOD

. To make pastry, rub butter into combined flour, baking powder and cinnamon. Add a little water and knead very lightly to a manageable dough. Set aside to cool.

. Place apples in slow cooker with 1 tablespoon water and all other filling ingredients and cook for around 3 hours on low or until apples are tender. Test apples from time to time. Remove cloves and if mixture is too wet, drain. Allow to cool.

. Preheat the oven to 200°C (400°F). Roll out the pastry on a floured board and cut out 10–12 pastry bases and the same numbers of tops. Line small, greased cupcake tins with pastry bases, spoon in a little filling, then press tops into place and make a vent hole in the crust. Bake for about 45 minutes.

. Sprinkle shorties with a little icing (confectioner's) sugar and serve either hot with cream as a dessert or cold as an afternoon treat.

CHERRY AND WALNUT FRUIT CAKE

MAKES 1 CAKE

INGREDIENTS

250 g (8 oz) butter

250 g (8 oz) brown sugar

5 eggs, beaten to a froth

500 g (1 lb) sultanas (golden raisins)

170 g (6 oz) glacé cherries

120 g (4 oz) walnut pieces

200 g (7 oz) plain (all-purpose) flour

15 ml (½ fl oz) milk

METHOD

. Cream the butter and sugar in a bowl. Add eggs gradually. Fold in fruit, walnuts and flour, then add milk.

. Grease a 23 cm (9 in) springform cake tin and line its sides and base with baking paper. Spoon in the cake mixture, cover and place in slow cooker. Cook on high for 4½–5 hours, taking care not to remove either the cooker or the cake tin lid until the last hour of cooking.

RICH BERRY DESSERT CAKE

SERVES 8

INGREDIENTS

120 g (4 oz) butter

¼ cup white sugar

1½ teaspoon vanilla extract

2 eggs, lightly beaten

2 cups plain (all-purpose) flour

2 teaspoons baking powder

salt

1 teaspoon mixed spice

125 ml (4 fl oz) milk

¾ cup berries of your choice

METHODS

. Cream the butter, sugar and vanilla, then fold eggs into mixture.

. Sift flour, baking powder and salt together and stir in mixed spice. Add spiced flour and milk alternately to the butter mixture, folding in gently and commencing and concluding with the flour. Spoon into a greased and floured 20 cm (8 in) springform cake tin, smooth the surface and arrange berries on top.

. Cover and place in slow cooker. Cook on high for approximately 3 hours, taking care not to remove either the cooker or the cake tin lid until the last hour of cooking. Sprinkle with cinnamon and icing (confectioner's) sugar and serve hot or cold, with thickened cream.

VIENNESE COFFEE CAKE

SERVES 8

INGREDIENTS

130 g (4½ oz) butter

¾ cup caster (superfine) sugar

½ teaspoon vanilla extract

3 eggs

1½ cups plain (all-purpose) flour, sifted

1½ teaspoons baking powder

pinch of salt

15 ml (½ fl oz) milk

COFFEE SYRUP

250 ml (8 floz) strong black coffee

⅓ cup raw sugar

30 ml (1 fl oz) brandy or whisky

METHOD

. Beat the butter until softened, then gradually beat in the sugar and vanilla until mixture is light and fluffy. Add eggs one at a time, beating well after each.

. Sift together flour, baking powder and salt and fold into butter mixture. Add milk – mixture should have a dropping consistency. Spoon into a greased 20 cm (8 in) springform cake tin, cover, and place tin in slow cooker. Cook on high for about 2–2½ hours, taking care not to remove either the cooker or the cake tin lid until the last 1 hour to 30 minutes of cooking time.

. Remove tin from slow cooker, allow to cool for about 10 minutes, then turn cake out of tin and allow to cool on a wire rack. When cold, replace in tin.

. To make the coffee syrup, place the coffee into a saucepan, add sugar and ⅔ cup water and heat until sugar dissolves. Add the brandy or whisky and bring to the boil, stirring occasionally. Boil for 3 minutes. Allow to cool.

. Pour cold syrup over cake and refrigerate overnight. Serve with cream.

DUNDEE MARMALADE PUDDING

SERVES 4–6

INGREDIENTS

500 ml (1 pint) milk

120 g (4 oz) fresh, fine breadcrumbs

3 eggs, separated

60 g (2 oz) caster (superfine) sugar

30 ml (1 fl oz) dark marmalade

METHOD

. Bring milk to the boil and pour over breadcrumbs. Allow to cool.

. Beat the egg yolks with the sugar, then add the marmalade. Stir into the cold bread and milk mixture. Beat the egg whites until stiff and fold in.

. Grease a pudding basin and lightly spoon in the pudding mixture. Cover basin tightly with foil and tie with kitchen string, forming a loop at the top so that the basin may be easily removed from the slow cooker. Place basin into cooker, pour over boiling water and cook on high for about 3 hours.

. Remove basin, carefully turn out pudding and serve with hot custard.

BANANAS IN RUM AND HONEY SYRUP

SERVES 4–6

INGREDIENTS

6 firm bananas, peeled
30 ml (1 fl oz) dark rum
15 ml (½ fl oz) honey
30 ml (1 fl oz) orange juice
juice of ½ lemon
½ teaspoon ground cinnamon

METHOD

. Arrange bananas in base of slow cooker. Combine rum, honey, juices and cinnamon and spoon over and around bananas. Cook on high for approximately ½–¾ hour or on low for approximately 1 hour, until bananas are just tender and syrup is heated through.

. Serve bananas with scoops of ice cream, with syrup spooned over.

LEMON SAGO PUDDING

SERVES 4

INGREDIENTS

1 cup uncooked sago

1 large egg

250 ml (8 fl oz) milk

1–2 tablespoons raw sugar

1 teaspoon vanilla extract

½ teaspoon ground nutmeg

zest of 1 lemon, grated

METHOD

. Bring 1 cup water to a fast boil and pour in the sago. Cook at a quick simmer, stirring often, until sago is translucent (about 15 minutes). If the water is absorbed before the sago is cooked, add a little more. When done, pour the sago into a bowl and allow to cool.

. Beat together the egg, milk and sugar in a bowl, then add remaining ingredients and sago. Pour mixture into a lightly greased dish, sprinkle with extra nutmeg and cover with a lid or foil.

. Place dish in the slow cooker, and carefully pour enough hot water around the dish to come three-quarters of the way up its sides. Cook on high for 2 hours or on low for 3 hours, then serve hot or cold with stewed fruit and whipped cream.

BAKED BREAD AND BUTTER PUDDING

SERVES 6

INGREDIENTS

4 thin slices stale brown or white
   bread, buttered

½ cup mixed sultanas (golden
   raisins) and currants

3 tablespoons raw sugar

½ teaspoon grated nutmeg or
   cinnamon

2 eggs

625 ml (1 pint 4 fl oz) milk

1 teaspoon vanilla extract

zest of ½ orange, grated

METHOD

. Remove crusts from bread and cut into thick fingers. Grease an
ovenproof dish and arrange bread in layers, buttered-side up.
Sprinkle layers with dried fruit, sugar and spice.

. Beat together eggs, milk and vanilla and stir in orange zest. Pour
mixture over layered bread and allow to stand for approximately 30
minutes. Cover dish with lid or foil.

. Pour 250 ml (8 fl oz) hot water into the slow cooker, then insert
the pudding dish and cook on high for 3–4 hours.

Index

First published in 2017 by New Holland Publishers
This edition published in 2022 by New Holland Publishers
Auckland • Sydney

newhollandpublishers.com

Level 1, 178 Fox Valley Road, Wahroonga 2076, Australia
5/39 Woodside Ave, Northcote, Auckland 0627, New Zealand

ISBN 9781760794637

Group Managing Director: Fiona Schultz
Designer: Yolanda La Gorcé
Production Director: Arlene Gippert

Printed in China

10 9 8 7 6 5 4 3 2 1

Keep up with New Holland Publishers:
f NewHollandPublishers
@newhollandpublishers

US $16.99